FAIR PLAY FOR FROGS

The Waldie-Frobish Papers

FAIR PLAY FOR FROGS

by Jerome R. Waldie and Nestle J. Frobish

HBJ

HARCOURT BRACE JOVANOVICH
New York and London

Printed in the United States of America

Library of Congress Cataloging in Publication Data

Waldie, Jerome R.
Fair play for frogs.
Includes index.
1. Frogs. 2. Wildlife conservation—California.
3. Statesmen—Correspondence. I. Frobish, Nes
Nestle J.m joint author. II. Title.
QL668.E2W26 1976 333.9'5 76-27418
ISBN 0-15-129961-7

First edition

B C D E

CONTENTS

Preface by Jerome R. Waldie

A subject as disturbing to me as the Worldwide Fair Play for Frogs Committee causes me to seek refuge in a total, protective loss of memory; nevertheless I will seek to dredge out of the black inner recesses of my mind my recollection as to how I first became entangled in its all encompassing web.

It started out, as do most tales of tragedy, quite innocently. In proper response to the plight of a constituent and his small child, I sought a legislative remedy to his problem.

My constituent was a sports editor of an influential weekly newspaper in my state assembly district. He also was a devotee of the slingshot, and a man who enjoyed frogs' legs as a culinary delight. One afternoon, while on an outing with his small child, he and the little one sought to satisfy both impulses by stunning frogs with slingshot pellets.

An official representative of the majestic State of California, a gamewarden, apprehended my constituent and his small child while they were engaged in this pursuit and charged them with a violation of one of California's little-noted laws, namely, the taking of frogs with slingshots.

Actually, no law prohibits the taking of frogs by slingshot, but no law permits it, either. If you desire to take frogs in California, you must do so by "gig" alone. A gig is a fearsome, cruel, forklike, barbed spear that impales a frog causing him great pain and suffering.

My constituent and I believed that a more humane approach to taking a frog would be to stun the latter with a slingshot pellet and thereafter to humanely and expeditiously reduce him or her to a state appropriate for cooking.

Accordingly, I introduced legislation to correct this absurd and contradictory situation. My assembly bill stated—in exquisite simplicity devoid of the usual superfluous rhetoric most politicians use in writing legislation—"Frogs may be taken by using a slingshot."

In truth and in retrospect, there was little discernible reaction to this forward-looking piece of Legislation—in part, I suspect, because of its direct approach to problem-solving, a disconcerting change from the usual legislative efforts.

But lurking in the swamp, so to speak, was the now painfully familiar impostor, Nestle J. Frobish. Seeking a vehicle, I suspect, to obtain funds from gullible friends of frogs, Nestle J. Frobish manufactured out of thin swamp mist the Fair Play for Frogs Committee. He used as a launching platform for his insidious machinations a rather gullible columnist noted in limited circles of the Bay Area for his ardent concern for bizarre causes, Art Hoppe. Nestle J. Frobish wrote Mr. Hoppe a rather idiotic and transparently false letter of concern for frogs and signed it as an officer of the Worldwide Fair Play for Frogs Committee. Mr. Hoppe, in the unique manner that accounts for his notoriety among a peculiar, small group of readers, published his letter, enabling Frobish to thereafter pretend to legitimacy.

J. R. W.
Bethesda, Md.

A Defiant Preface by Nestle J. Frobish

At the age of thirty-one I was still an idealistic, happy-go-lucky lad, meaning harm to no one, optimistic, enthusiastic, not yet exposed to the awful fact that Evil was afoot in the land. My greatest pleasure was to sit about in the evening and listen to the gentle croaking of man's humble friend and servant, the frog. But on March 21, 1961, my rural reverie was shattered by soul-wrenching news. One Jerome R. Waldie, a man of whom neither I nor millions of other good citizens had ever heard, rose in the assembly of the great state of California to launch his now notorious anti-frog crusade.

"We must allow the taking of frogs by slingshot," thundered this flagitious wretch.

From that day my life was changed. No longer good-natured, devil-may-care "Ned" Frobish, I donned the armor of righteousness and founded the Worldwide Fair Play for Frogs Committee. "The forces of evil," I declared to anyone who would listen, "must be thwarted. And in particular, Jerome R. Waldie, the Mad Butcher of the Swamps, must be defeated!"

In the fourteen years since that fateful day my best efforts have been unswervingly dedicated to either reforming this Waldie, or failing that, destroying his career. It saddens my heart to relate the perfidy and iniquity of this blackguard! His honeyed words, his deceiving smile! His guile, his protestations of innocence! But through all his manifold tergiversations, Jerome R. Waldie has relentlessly pursued the central purpose of his benighted existence, to wit, the extermination of Frogdom throughout the world.

The correspondence that portrays our activities over

A DEFIANT PREFACE

these fourteen years forms the subject of this book. You may well inquire how I could permit my name to be published on the same title page with that of this modern Moloch. Indeed, it was with reluctance that I eventually succumbed to the entreaties of our good publisher. But finally it dawned on me that the whole sordid story must be brought to the attention of the public. "Let the people be the judge!" I exclaimed in a sudden moment of perceptivity, and the rest is history.

This is not a book that can be read at one sitting. Not that it is not of great morbid interest; but a decent, civilized reader can usually only absorb so much wickedness at one time, and the exhibition of wickedness and deceit purveyed by my (and I blush to say it) coauthor is a heavy, heavy dose. I am confident, however, that the exposure of this whole episode to the humane public will bring forth such a storm of pro-frog protest, that whatever Waldie's goals may be henceforth, the persecution of frogs may no longer be among them.

My share of the proceeds of this book will be devoted to the pro-frog cause that I have so long championed. Waldie may use his share as he sees fit—he insisted on that—but I want to reiterate once again that his use of a portion of it for competent psychiatric attention would be most appropriate.

N. J. F.
Lyndonville, Vt.

Introduction to
THE WALDIE-FROBISH PAPERS
by Morris K. Udall

Rarely in my experience have I had the responsibility, perchance the opportunity, to participate in an undertaking that has so little bearing on the affairs of state as the Waldie-Frobish Papers.

But, the sheer inconsequence of the exchange of correspondence between these individuals is the genius of the work.

Indeed, what might appear as frivolous letters to some will be heady stuff to others.

What is remarkable in Jerome Waldie's case is that he was able to disengage himself from his serious efforts as California's Assembly Majority Leader and later as a respected and effective Member of Congress to devote the time and effort to answer the letters of one Nestle J. Frobish, himself reputed to be occupied in matters of some import.

In reading their correspondence, I think it was time well spent by both.

Having labored myself in the House of Representatives for some fifteen years and having pursued my party's presidential nomination, I have more than a casual acquaintance with the value of diversion, the merit of wit, if not the worth of frogs.

All which leads to an incident in New Hampshire during the 1976 primary campaign and thus far unnoticed by the chroniclers of politics, an event involving Mr. Waldie, Mr. Frobish, and my fellow candidate Jimmy Carter, an event that has remained uncovered too long.

INTRODUCTION

Mr. Carter, as many will recall, was making a strong effort to wrest the all-important New Hampshire primary victory from my grasp. In the midst of this heated campaign came one of the most inflammatory of the political carpetbaggers of this age, Carter's fellow Georgian, Lester Maddox.

Maddox wasn't in the chilly climes of New Hampshire more than thirty minutes when he aimed a sackful of charges of deceit and deception at his former running mate.

Carter's response, issued by an aide, was one of the best pieces of political repartee of the campaign.

Said he, "Being called a liar by Lester Maddox is like being called ugly by a frog."

At the very time of the Carter response I was campaigning in New Hampshire and neighboring Vermont, which was also to hold an early spring primary.

That night my campaign advance person summoned me to a hand-crank telephone in downtown Contoocook's finest hostelry telling me that my old House colleague and friend Jerry Waldie was on the telephone in a very excitable state.

"No!" shouted the usually unflappable Waldie, "I've the secret to winning the Vermont primary and very possibly the nomination itself!"

Naturally interested, I asked him to continue.

"Carter's made an egregious error. He's aroused the pro-frog vote and Frobish will nail him good!"

"Frobish?" I replied. "What's a frobish—is it contagious?"

INTRODUCTION

His patience taxed to the limit, Waldie roared, "Frobish is a he—an unreckoned major power in American politics. You ought to know what he did to me in 1974. Single-handedly he wrecked my own campaign for governor of California allowing Jerry Brown to edge me out by several hundred thousand votes."

"Well, what should I do with this Frobish person," said I.

Waldie, showing that he had prepared well for this call, reeled off a calculated political strategy aimed at exploiting what he called "a purposeful slight at all of American amphibianry—Ranas purity, if you will."

Waldie suggested "an immediate denunciation of Carter and the hiring of Frobish as a key campaign aide. Follow this with a dramatic news conference at Frobish's model swamp in Lyndonville, Vermont, his winter home.

"Do these things, Udall, and you can't miss," Waldie assured me. "This Frobish is a real power."

As was usually the case in my presidential campaign, I was torn.

Should I accept the advice of a veteran and knowledgeable politician, a man who was one of the legitimate heroes of the House Judiciary Committee's impeachment proceedings, or should I continue my campaign as before, forcefully debating the issues of inflation, unemployment, governmental reform, and the dental floss tariff?

After some thought, not too much, but some, I chose to politely decline Waldie's advice.

I did not contact Nestle J. Frobish.

INTRODUCTION

And, Jimmy Carter kicked my ass in New Hampshire and all around the nation.*

It is of little solace to now realize that Waldie and Udall are not the only political figures undone by Frobish.

However, there is comfort in being asked to preface the product of the unusual minds of Waldie and Frobish and to pocket the modest fee exacted from the two for the honor.

It might be well to mention at this point that all is not well in the relationship of the authors of this book.

In fact, one is reminded of an exchange between two other would-be authors, Winston Churchill and George Bernard Shaw.

Shaw invited Churchill by letter to the opening night of his newest play.

"Hope you will come and I enclose two tickets so that you may bring a friend—if you have one."

To which Churchill replied, "I received your kind invitation and the tickets. Matters of state will prevent me from attending the opening and I am returning the tickets. However, I would appreciate two tickets for the second night's performance—if there is one."

I have more to say about Waldie and Frobish; however, I will save my comments for the preface to the second edition—if there is one.

—Mo Udall

* If in the interest of taste the reference to "ass" in the above paragraph outrages Frobish or his agents—substitute "posterior" or some other anatomical reference.

FAIR PLAY FOR FROGS

ASSEMBLY BILL No. 2301

Introduced by Mr. Waldie

March 21, 1961

REFERRED TO COMMITTEE ON FISH AND GAME

An act to add Section 6856 to the Fish and
Game Code, relating to frogs.

The people of the State of California do enact as follows:

1 SECTION 1. Section 6856 is added to the Fish and Game
2 Code, to read:
3 6856. Frogs may be taken by using a slingshot.

LEGISLATIVE COUNSEL'S DIGEST
A.B. 2301, as introduced, Waldie (F. & G.). Frogs.
Adds Sec. 0856, F. & G.C.
Authorizes the use of slingshots to take frogs.

Berkeley 4, California
December 17, 1961

Mr. Art Hoppe
San Francisco Chronicle
San Francisco, California

Dear Mr. Hoppe:

I read your columns with great interest and agree with
you fully that things are really. But be that as it may, I
feel compelled to bring to your attention a shocking rev-
elation—so shocking, in fact, that I am almost ashamed
to be an American:

THE UNITED STATES HAS NEVER ACCEPTED THE 1899
CONVENTION AGAINST DUMDUM BULLETS!!

These bullets, as you may know, are bullets which

FAIR PLAY FOR FROGS

expand or flatten easily in the human body, causing serious damage to any organs or parts that happen to lie in the way. Fenwick, in his work on international law, tells us that

> These bullets, known as dumdum bullets, after the arsenal near Calcutta where they were first made, were introduced by the British as a means of putting out of action Indians who could not be stopped by the use of ordinary bullets.

Indeed, in those early days it might have seemed necessary to reserve the right to use such bullets, since three hundred years of warfare may not have proved definitively that most soldiers can be stopped by ordinary bullets. However, in the last seventy years a great wealth of empirical data has been built up to the effect that ordinary bullets can stop almost anyone that one wishes to stop, when aimed judiciously. Not only this, but new and even more effective methods have been devised for the same purpose, like nerve gas, vaporization, and itch powder.

In view of all this, I think it is imperative for our government to forswear once and for all the use of dumdum bullets in international war. It would be a magnificent unilateral beginning for disarmament, and the Russians could be invited to reciprocate. We should do this right away, for in a few years the despised Red Chinese may have dumdum bullets of their own, thus adding a sinister new dimension to international tension. As a leading publicist, I hope you will bring this serious situation to the attention of your many influential readers.

Yours truly,

Nestle J. Frobish

Nestle J. Frobish,
East Bay Committee to
Outlaw Dumdum Bullets

San Francisco Chronicle

January 3, 1962

Dear Mr. Frobish:

I happen to be the nephew of the owner of the Hot Damn Dum-Dum Bullet Company. And I consider your outrageous attack on these missiles of mercy a base canard.

But in fairness I plan to write a column embodying your ridiculous ideas. If you have any more will you send them to me? Columns are hard to come by.

Outrageously yours,

Art Hoppe

Mr. Nestle J. Frobish
Berkeley, California

March 9, 1962

Art Hoppe
San Francisco Chronicle
San Francisco, California

Hoppe, you scoundrel:

Well, I sure made my mistake by writing *you* about the dumdum bullet menace. How was I to know you were in the employ of the Hot Damn people? Ordinarily, I would turn my back on you and go see Burton Wolfe with new facts on the threat of corporate power, but now I need your help.

You no doubt have read about the Monster that some scientists discovered on a Tasmanian beach a few days

FAIR PLAY FOR FROGS

ago. Now I have an idea that may make us a pile of money. Wouldn't that be good? Certainly. So listen.

I sent the enclosed letter to the scientist in charge of this expedition. If this deal goes through, I can stake the little monster out in the Berkeley Yacht Harbor and charge for rides for the kiddies, etc. The only investment needed is a little postage and handling and a ticket booth. We can throw the booth together out of orange crates.

All you have to do is drum up some publicity and you get a healthy cut of the profits. And it's practically all profit. All monster has to do for food is scavenge around the bay a little. Even the attendant won't cost much—I'm getting a Bigfoot to sell tickets, and I think they are exempt from the minimum wage laws.

Please let me know right away if you will cooperate.

Yours truly,

Nestle J. Frobish
Berkeley, California

San Francisco Chronicle

San Francisco Chronicle
March, 1962

A Monster on the Beach

Hobart, Tasmania

March 3 (AP)—Australian scientists are puzzled by a huge carcass found on a remote beach on the west coast of Tasmania.

FAIR PLAY FOR FROGS

They say it is like no known creature.

It is circular in shape and has no eyes, no defined head and no bone structure. Its creamy, rubbery flesh is probably 12 inches thick and covered with woolly hair.

The monster is 20 feet long, 18 feet wide and 4½ feet thick and weighs between five and 10 tons.

It is described as like a huge turtle without appendages.

Scientist Bruce Hollison of the Commonwealth Scientific and Industrial Research Organization was in an expedition that made a hazardous trek to the scene this week.

He said the monster's characteristics appeared to be different from all larger known fish or sea mammals.

"I believe the creature is an animal but it is unlike anything I have seen or heard of," he said.

"It could be new in the animal kingdom," said G. Whitely, curator of fishes at the Australian Museum.

March 9, 1962

Dr. Bruce Hollison
Commonwealth Scientific and Industrial
Research Organization
Sydney, Australia

Dear Dr. Hollison:

According to recent Associated Press reports, you are the discoverer of a giant rubbery, hairy, boneless monster on a Tasmanian Beach.

Do you suppose you could poke around in it and see if it has any babies available? I would like very much to have one, and would pay all postage and handling charges.

FAIR PLAY FOR FROGS

I promise to take very good care of it, and feed and comb it regularly.

Yours truly,

Nestle J Frobish

N. J. Frobish
Berkeley, California

San Francisco Chronicle

March 14, 1962

Dear Nestle (if I may):

I am starting a collection to be entitled "The Uncollected Letters of Nestle J. Frobish." Your last was a masterpiece.

Unfortunately, by the time I got back from Washington, it was a little out of date or I would have stolen it for a column. Send more, send more.

Monstrously yours,

Art Hoppe

Art Hoppe

Mr. Nestle J. Frobish
Berkeley, California

FAIR PLAY FOR FROGS

March 20, 1962

Dear Art,

Well, I just found out that if we good citizens turn our back even for an instant, he'll run amok, destroying any defenseless creature in his path. Assemblyman Waldie, I mean. From up around Antioch.

To while away the time until our Monster arrives from Tasmania, I puttered around trying to find out if there were any state regulations governing the required care of monsters, et al., when I found it. A. B. 2301. Waldie's anti-frog bill (enclosed). And I'm not sure how to fight it.

You see, if I write him and protest his bill on the grounds that the courts may stretch the law to permit hordes of vandals to come down to the yacht harbor to pelt Monster with stones from slingshots, the cat, or whatever it is, will be out of the bag, or whatever it's in. So our only recourse is to oppose the bill on the grounds that it is unfair to the frog, mankind's friend, vernal harbinger of rebirth, etc.

So I've dug up the old mailing list of the Committee to Oppose the Hunting of the Passenger Pigeon by Garotte, which apparently flourished here for some years until the piano-wire industry managed to crush it, and have reformed it into the East Bay Committee for Fair Play to Frogs and Justice for Morton Sobell. Actually, I don't give a damn about Morton Sobell but the people who were willing to join the Fair Play for Frogs Committee would only do so if I included the Sobell bit. But I'm trying to play that down.

So we've started a mammoth letter campaign to force the infamous Waldie to withdraw this bill. Get everybody over there to join in, Art. Remember, the hand that holds the slingshot ruins our whole scheme. He must fail! If

FAIR PLAY FOR FROGS

Waldie can beat the EBC for FP to F and J for MS, we are undone. The forces are joined, and the outcome is in the hands of God. And in this case I think it is safe to encourage the notion that we are his agents on earth. This is a good line I have used before. Like, go all out.

Yours in distress,

Nestle

Nestle

Berkeley, California
March 20, 1962

Hon. Jerome Waldie
State Capitol
Sacramento, California

Dear Assemblyman Waldie:

I am writing to oppose vigorously your bill, A. B. 2301, which would permit the taking of frogs by slingshot.

The frog is, by nature, a friendly creature. We do not hear of bands of wild frogs carrying off children. We do not hear of rabies being caused by the bite of a maddened frog. Frogs have never been known to proliferate to the point where, like the Australian rabbit, they pose a threat to the well-being of settlers.

Rather, the frog crouches amiably in his aqueous lair, asking only the opportunity to go his unmolested way, and giving in return the pleasant chuggarum of an evening to the true nature lover, of which there are many and all of whom vote.

It is deplorable enough that man, the intruder, has sought to depopulate the frog community thru various existing legal methods. Now comes along a callous politi-

FAIR PLAY FOR FROGS

cian like you—no doubt in the clutches of the notorious sportsman's lobby—who would add one more weapon to the terrible array now used by man to crush the inoffensive frog.

Legalize slingshots, I say, and one more giant step will have been taken toward the ultimate rape of frogdom. What next? Soon the "sportsmen" will demand the legalization of flamethrowers, napalm, and poison gas. I say the time has come to draw the line once and for all on this matter. Spare the humble frog the anguish of further oppression. Withdraw this noxious bill from the assembly agenda.

Yours,

Nestle J. Frobish

Nestle J. Frobish
Fair Play for Frogs Committee
East Bay Chapter

LAW OFFICES
113 G STREET
ANTIOCH. CALIFORNIA
TELEPHONE PL 7-4545

SACRAMENTO ADDRESS
STATE CAPITOL
ZONE 14

COMMITTEES
EDUCATION
FINANCE AND INSURANCE
JUDICIARY
WAYS AND MEANS

Assembly
California Legislature

JEROME R. WALDIE
ASSEMBLYMAN. TENTH DISTRICT
CONTRA COSTA COUNTY

MAJORITY FLOOR LEADER

March 23, 1962

Mr. Nestle J. Frobish
Fair Play for Frogs Committee
Berkeley, California

Dear Mr. Frobish:

The Fair Play for Frogs Committee, which you purport to represent, has, in an estimable and commendable display of overenthusiasm and overcompassion, completely misconstrued the purposes of Assembly Bill 2301.

In fact, the purposes and aims of this legislation can and should be ardently endorsed and supported by your group.

Apparently you are unaware of the present law relative to "taking of frogs." The present statutes permit, and even encourage, the taking of frogs by an instrument known as a gig.

A gig is a three-pronged fork with barbs on each point designed to impale the amiable frog. You can scarcely conceive a more barbarous instrument.

Recognition of these unhappy facts prompted me to introduce a bill to permit the taking of frogs by a more humane method, namely, stunning the frog by a smooth pellet launched by a slingshot.

I was initiated into this project by a constituent who had sought to utilize this more humane method, but was prevented from doing so by existing law.

The status of this legislation at present date can best be described as uncertain.

Despite an impassioned plea before the Fish and Game Committee outlining the incontrovertible facts referred to herein, the members of that committee did not see fit to report the bill out.

Consequently, the bill remains in committee and has been there for approximately one year to date.

I do not believe there is great enthusiasm for this endeavor beyond the narrow confines of the constituent who sought the introduction of the bill.

Unless an organized pressure group such as the Fair Play for Frogs Committee makes this a project of their very own, I reluctantly conclude the prospects for ultimate success are indeed dim.

I urge your consideration of undertaking this campaign in furtherance of Fair Play for Frogs.

Cordially yours,

Jerome R. Waldie

JRW:cl

San Francisco Chronicle

March 27, 1962

OUR MAN HOPPE
MR. JEROME WALDIE, FRIEND OF FROGS
Art Hoppe

My friend, Mr. N. J. Frobish of Berkeley, the Outraged Liberal, has taken vigorous and positive action in behalf of his latest cause. He's written another letter.

Mr. Frobish, you recall, became outraged this time by Assemblyman Jerome Waldie's bill (A. B. 2301), which says: "Frogs may be taken by using a slingshot." So Mr. Frobish formed The East Bay Committee for Fair Play to Frogs and Morton Sobell. (He says he just threw Mr. Sobell in to broaden the scope of the membership.) And he has now written a letter of outrage to Mr. Waldie.

I quote: "The frog is, by nature, a friendly creature. We do not hear of bands of wild frogs carrying off children. We do not hear of rabies being caused by the bite of a maddened frog. . . . Rather, the frog crouches amiably in his aqueous lair, asking only the opportunity to go his unmolested way, and giving in return the pleasant chug-garum of an evening to the true nature lover, *of which there are many and all of whom vote.*"

Mr. Frobish then accuses Mr. Waldie of being "a callous politician," a tool of "the notorious sportsman's lobby" and demands he cease this "rape of frogdom."

I felt this was such a classic case of Outraged Liberalism on the rampage that I checked with Mr. Waldie, who is the Democrats' young and able majority floor leader in the assembly. And also very likable.

"I am a misunderstood man," said Mr. Waldie sadly. "Actually, I am a well-known friend of frogs. My bill was a purely humanitarian endeavor and I made an emotional and impassioned plea for it before the Fish and Game Committee.

"As I explained to them, frog hunters presently take frogs by gigging. A gig is a three-pronged spear. With barbs. It goes in, snickety-snack, and is pulled out, snackety-snick . . . Horrible! I hoped that authorizing humane slingshot pellets would act as a moral force to reform giggers. Unfortunately, the committee was unmoved and failed even to refer my bill to interim study."

Mr. Waldie thoughtfully detailed all this in a letter back to Mr. Frobish, of which I have a copy. It winds up: "Unless an organized pressure group such as the Fair Play for Frogs Committee makes this a project of their very own, I reluctantly conclude the prospects for ultimate success are indeed dim. I urge your consideration of undertaking this campaign in furtherance of Fair Play for Frogs."

Frankly, I doubt Mr. Waldie will get much help from Mr. Frobish, now that the facts are known. Outraged Liberals, I've noticed, seldom get outraged *in favor* of anything.

I'm glad to report, however, in wrapping up this classic case, that Mr. Waldie's humanitarianism hasn't gone unrewarded. His fellow legislators have presented him with a bronze plaque.

Who could help but be moved by the simple Latin inscription? Ranas Curant Deus et Waldie. Which, freely translated, means: "Only the Good Lord and Waldie give

FAIR PLAY FOR FROGS

a hang about frogs." And if you ask me, that takes care of Mr. Frobish, the Outraged Liberal.

March 27, 1962

Dear Art,

Your (our) campaign to bring the Truth to the American people is off to a fine beginning. The only trouble is, I am a little perplexed by the attitude of Assemblyman Waldie on all this. See enclosed letter.

On one hand, he is apparently not exactly "running amok" in his intent to destroy frogdom. The judicious tone of his reply to me indicates that he is, at least, not on the verge of commitment to an institution.

On the other hand, although he stoutly defends his bill to legalize the slingshooting of frogs as a humane measure that is deserving of the support of all frog-lovers, he cleverly does not proceed to the logical conclusion—that a bill should be introduced outlawing the taking of frogs by gigs.

In any case, our original clandestine purpose in opposing this legislation seems to be in sight of victory. That is when Monster arrives, it will be illegal for local toughs to pelt him (it?) (them?) with slingshot stones. I am not at all concerned about the possibility of anyone trying to take the Monster with a gig. Such a gig would indeed have to be a marvel. I calculate that a gig sufficient to capture a Monster 20′ x 30′, and 4.5′ thick, would rise to the height of a nine-story building. So anyway, the threat to Monster, and hence to our fortunes, is negligible so long as the Fish and Game Committee sits tight on Waldie's bill.

In view of this, I feel a little sorry for Mr. Waldie. Now he will have to explain his position on the frog issue to thousands of tenth-district voters next November. An unscrupulous opponent could parlay any false step by Waldie into his defeat. It is sometimes strange and marvelous how an issue as seemingly insignificant as the frog slingshot bill might change the course of history. At least in the tenth district. I am certain that Mr. Waldie will think long and deep before introducing any further legislation. Such is the power of the press and Outraged Liberals.

I'll let you know as soon as I get word from Tasmania.

Yours,

Nestle

Nestle

PS: I blush to bring this up, Art, but on reading and rereading your column in today's Chronicle, I thought, but of course I could be mistaken, that there was, but of course, maybe there really wasn't, a slight, but not too noticeable, of course, air of—how to say it?—frivolity? in the tone of your remarks. I'm sure that you agree that we must make every effort to keep our crusade above the level of common amusement.

NJF

April 2, 1962

Hon. Jerome Waldie
State Capitol
Sacramento, California

Dear Mr. Waldie:

Your clever explanations, coupled with the power of the Bought Press, has done its evil work. Here in Berkeley your name is on everyone's lips as Defender of the Ami-

FAIR PLAY FOR FROGS

able Frog. Your fellow legislators, according to one San Francisco journalist, have awarded you the coveted Friend of Frogs Plaque for 1962. I understand that Calaveras County, by motion of the Board of Supervisors, is preparing a memorial to you. Truly, you are at the pinnacle of your legislative career.

In your hour of triumph what can one crushed, scorned Outraged Liberal say? I say that when the smoke has cleared, the shouting crowds retired to their homes, the paeans of the Press subsided—what will be left?

Only the stark, sober fact that Waldie found another way to murder the amiable Frog.

Assassin!

But my cause is lost, at least among the grassroots. My Fair Play for Frogs Committee, gulled into accepting— indeed, preconizing—your new Image, has abandoned this case for other projects.

Only the self-effacing, dedicated, gallant members of the Fish and Game Committee hold the line. Bless them all.

I hope that someday, when you find yourself strolling down some bucolic lane and the pleasant chuggarum of the friendly frog delights your heart, you will rethink deeply your present course—that you will take courage, return to the Assembly floor, and demand that California be made safe for frogs once and for all!

Until then, I remain,

Yours truly,

Nestle J. Frobish

Nestle J. Frobish
Outraged Liberal

JEROME R. WALDIE
MEMBER OF CONGRESS
14TH DISTRICT, CALIFORNIA

WASHINGTON ADDRESS:
ROOM 408
CANNON HOUSE OFFICE BUILDING
WASHINGTON, D.C. 20515
PHONE: 225-5911
AREA CODE: 202

COMMITTEES:
JUDICIARY
POST OFFICE AND CIVIL SERVICE
SELECT COMMITTEE ON CRIME

DISTRICT REPRESENTATIVE:
E. A. "PAT" FERGUSON
P.O. BOX 864
CIVIC CENTER
CONCORD, CALIFORNIA 94520
PHONE: 687-1200
AREA CODE: 415

RICHMOND OFFICE:
3915 MACDONALD AVENUE
RICHMOND, CALIFORNIA 94805
PHONE: 233-4425

Congress of the United States
House of Representatives
Washington, D.C. 20515

May 14, 1969

Mr. Nestle J. Frobish
Lyndonville, Vermont

Dear Mr. Frobish:

Had my measure permitting the taking of frogs with a slingshot been passed, the tragedy exhibited by the headline you forwarded me concerning the demise of bullfrogs might not have occurred. In fact, assuming that most sportsmen are as inaccurate in their use of a slingshot as I, I am inclined to believe that this vital source would have not only been maintained but would have increased immeasurably.

I was interested in your having moved from the West Coast and taken up residence in Lyndonville. I knew there were a few Democrats who were so disturbed by the announcement of President Johnson that he would not be a candidate for election that they would go to

FAIR PLAY FOR FROGS

extreme ends to express their loyalty to him. However, few have gone as far as have you in that demonstration.

Sincerely yours,

Jerry Waldie

JEROME R. WALDIE
United States Congressman
Fourteenth District

JRW:bsr

Lyndonville, Vermont 05851
June 4, 1969

Hon. Jerome Waldie
House Office Building
Washington, D.C.

Dear Mr. Waldie:

Why dissimulate? If your goal in life was to protect and advance the cause of frogs, as you so righteously assert, you would have introduced legislation to outlaw the use of gigs which, as you point out with scarcely suppressed relish, really do a job on a frog, snickety snick, snickety snack.

Not only did you *not* challenge the gig lobby, you appeased the slingshot lobby. Not only did you *not* act to protect the amiable genus Rana, you fought to legalize one more way of committing ranacide. While outlawing gigs and legalizing slingshots would have been some improvement, attributable to the diminished efficacy of the latter, you didn't even do that. Let's face it. You have got it in for frogs, Waldie. Why not come out and say it—at least be an honest man about it.

My opinion of the late Lyndon Johnson, to which you

FAIR PLAY FOR FROGS

allude in what appears to be an opiate-sodden flight of fancy, is that slingshots should be legalized in hunting him, not to mention a number of other items which I refrain from naming only because you would most likely try to turn them against frogs. I am a fierce Republican, Hoppe's characterization's to the contrary notwithstanding. If the rest of us Republicans stand up for the rights of the frog the way I have, against formidable and entrenched opposition, we may once again be the majority party in this country. I wish the President would lay off the silly ABM thing and get with this.

Contumaciously,

Nestle J. Frobish

Nestle J. Frobish

FAIR PLAY FOR FROGS

JEROME R. WALDIE
MEMBER OF CONGRESS
14TH DISTRICT, CALIFORNIA

WASHINGTON ADDRESS:
ROOM 406
CANNON HOUSE OFFICE BUILDING
WASHINGTON, D.C. 20515
PHONE: 225-5511
AREA CODE: 202

COMMITTEES:
JUDICIARY
POST OFFICE AND CIVIL SERVICE
SELECT COMMITTEE ON CRIME

DISTRICT REPRESENTATIVE:
E. A. "PAT" FERGUSON
P.O. BOX 864
CIVIC CENTER
CONCORD, CALIFORNIA 94520
PHONE: 687-1200
AREA CODE: 415

RICHMOND OFFICE:
3915 MACDONALD AVENUE
RICHMOND, CALIFORNIA 94805
PHONE: 233-4425

Congress of the United States
House of Representatives
Washington, D.C. 20515

June 14, 1969

Mr. Nestle J. Frobish
Lyndonville, Vermont 05851

Dear Mr. Frobish:

I have received your interesting letter of June 4th, 1969, and have carefully read its contents.

In the event the matters discussed by you in that letter come before me for a vote, you may be assured that your views will receive my full and complete consideration.

Sincerely yours,

Jerry Waldie

JEROME R. WALDIE
United States Congressman
Fourteenth District

JRW:mrr

FAIR PLAY FOR FROGS

Lyndonville, Vt. 05851
March 12, 1970

"Hon." Jerome Waldie
House Office Building
Washington, DC

Dear Frogslayer:
Outraged frog-lovers from as far away as Mexico City,
Dallas, and Rutland, Vermont, have been incensed by the
enclosed AP wirephoto pictures of California policemen
using slingshots to assassinate frogs by the thousands.
Oh yes, I know the caption says they are pelting rioters,
but I know the glassy-eyed look of a ranacide when I see
one, and that cop has it.
I just hope you have a twinge of conscience for lending
your prestigious support to this outrage in your native
state. If reading "The Murder of the Frogs," which I sent
you in the hope its message would seep through any
hidden fissure to your vestigial sense of justice and fair
play, did not motivate you to repent, perhaps these ghastly
pictures will do so.
A more petty man than I, Nestle J. Frobish, would long
ago have consigned you to the flames, Waldie. But, as a
true Outraged Liberal, so called, I can never quite bring
myself to the point to write you off as an utterly hopeless
proposition. But my magnanimity does have limits. Don't
push me too far.
Yours for improving the quality of life for frogs as well
as people especially since people have a better chance,
Nestle J. Frobish
Nestle J. Frobish, President
Worldwide Fair Play for Frogs Committee

JEROME R. WALDIE
MEMBER OF CONGRESS
14TH DISTRICT, CALIFORNIA

WASHINGTON ADDRESS:
ROOM 408
CANNON HOUSE OFFICE BUILDING
WASHINGTON, D.C. 20515
PHONE: 225-5511
AREA CODE: 202

COMMITTEES:
JUDICIARY
POST OFFICE AND CIVIL SERVICE
SELECT COMMITTEE ON CRIME

DISTRICT REPRESENTATIVE:
E. A. "PAT" FERGUSON
P.O. BOX 864
CIVIC CENTER
CONCORD, CALIFORNIA 94520
PHONE: 687-1200
AREA CODE: 415

RICHMOND OFFICE:
3915 MACDONALD AVENUE
RICHMOND, CALIFORNIA 94805
PHONE: 233-4425

Congress of the United States
House of Representatives
Washington, D.C. 20515

March 30, 1970

Mr. Nestle J. Frobish, President
Worldwide Fair Play for Frogs Committee
Lyndonville, Vermont 05851

Dear Mr. Frobish:

I believe I will write J. Edgar Hoover, our beloved Director of the FBI, and call to his attention your peculiar and probably subversive activities.

I have, frankly, long suspected you of possessing tendencies inimical to 100% Americanism, but your latest defense of rioters really disturbs me.

Probably you already have a file in Director Hoover's office, but believe me, I could—and probably will—add a few pages to it.

Frogs, indeed! Your concerns aren't with frogs—I'm just beginning to understand the depth of your conspiracy, and I am wise to you.

Besides, your reference to improving the "quality of life for people" is really a tip-off.

I'm wise to you, Frobish.

Sincerely yours,

JEROME R. WALDIE
United States Congressman
Fourteenth District

JRW/ml

Lyndonville, Vermont 05851
June 17, 1970

Mr. Charles Peters, Editor
Washington Monthly
Washington, D. C. 20036

Dear Mr. Peters:

Your June article *Obstacles to Reform: Nobody Covers the House,* recently brought to my attention, describes Rep. Jerome Waldie as "an obscure, previously conservative and well-behaved" two-term Congressman from California. This description reveals a woeful ignorance on the part of the writer as to Mr. Waldie's nefarious background.

While a member of the California Assembly, prior to arriving in Congress, Mr. Waldie, though perhaps deserving some claim to obscurity, was anything but conservative and well behaved. In fact, he was the utterly radical and unscrupulous tool of the sportsman's lobby, as exemplified by his sponsorship of the notorious anti-environ-

FAIR PLAY FOR FROGS

ment, pro-violence A. B. 2301, the Waldie Frog-Murder Bill.

In case this monstrous piece of legislation has escaped the attention of your readers, it is worthwhile to quote it in its entirety:

"Frogs may be taken by using a slingshot."

It was not enough that countless methods already existed for harassing the amiable frog; Waldie, in the clutches of blood-thirsty frog murderers, fought fiercely to add yet another. With slingshots legitimized as an instrument of ranacide, it was clear what would be next—flamethrowers and nerve gas. Fortunately, the assembly in its wisdom let Waldie's Frog-Murder Bill languish in committee, despite what he himself has termed his impassioned pleas for its adoption. The moral to this story is, before inventing a new hero, check into his dark and bloody past.

Yours truly,

Nestle J. Frobish

Nestle J. Frobish
Chairman
Worldwide Fair Play for Frogs Committee

JEROME R. WALDIE
MEMBER OF CONGRESS
14TH DISTRICT, CALIFORNIA

WASHINGTON ADDRESS:
ROOM 408
CANNON HOUSE OFFICE BUILDING
WASHINGTON, D.C. 20515
PHONE: 225-5511
AREA CODE: 202

COMMITTEES:
JUDICIARY
POST OFFICE AND CIVIL SERVICE
SELECT COMMITTEE ON CRIME

DISTRICT REPRESENTATIVE:
E. A. "PAT" FERGUSON
P.O. Box 864
CIVIC CENTER
CONCORD, CALIFORNIA 94520
PHONE: 687-1200
AREA CODE: 415

RICHMOND OFFICE:
3915 MACDONALD AVENUE
RICHMOND, CALIFORNIA 94805
PHONE: 233-4425

Congress of the United States
House of Representatives
Washington, D.C. 20515

July 14, 1970

Mr. Nestle J. Frobish, Chairman
Worldwide Fair Play for Frogs Committee
Lyndonville, Vermont 05851

Dear Mr. Frobish:

The WASHINGTON MONTHLY has brought to my attention your latest letter of harassment.

I have yet to find an individual as hung up on frogs as are you.

I am consulting Freud's works as well as several competent psychiatrists to determine the full meaning of this unnatural attachment.

By the way, and apropos of nothing, you may have missed an event that casts great doubts on your continual assertions that I am less than beloved by frog-lovers—an odious group at best.

That event was a Sacramento gathering of these rather weird people where I was presented with a remarkable testament to my efforts on their behalf. I have received, midst thunderous ovations, a plaque which I have before me that reproduced my landmark legislation in its entirety and the engraving says:

Jerome R. Waldie

Ranas Curant Deus et Waldie.

Perhaps this will cause you to desist from your intemperate efforts to diminish my generally pleasant image with the public at large.

Sincerely yours,

Jerry Waldie

JEROME R. WALDIE, M. C.

JRW:mrr

NESTLE J. FROBISH

Lyndonville, Vermont 05851

March 14, 1970

Jerome R. Waldie, M. C.

House Office Building

Washington, D. C. 20515

Dear Mr. Waldie:

I have consulted my files on your activities over the past decade, which will form an important part of my forthcoming best seller "Frogdom Through the Ages," and do indeed find apocryphal mention of an award allegedly received by a person described as being you, for your supposed benevolence to genus Rana.

Unfortunately, the circumstances surrounding this report make it about as credible as the Cardiff Giant and the Lost Continent of Lemuria. In the first place, it was authored

FAIR PLAY FOR FROGS

by the notorious Arthur Hoppe, and it is well known that no one can believe anything Hoppe sets on paper. West Vhhthng, indeed! General Hoo Got Gum? Poppycock. Furthermore, Hoppe cannot be considered a disinterested reporter, even if he should accidentally report the truth. I myself entered an abortive business venture with him, to be entitled "Art and Frobe's Monster Rides," a children's attraction in the Berkeley Yacht Harbor featuring a nondescript monster that some years ago washed up on a Tasmanian beach. I immediately terminated this relationship when I discovered in Hoppe the same dark trait so manifest in you—an insane desire to persecute amphibians.

Finally, the Hoppe report, also alleged by you, is false on its face. How could there have been any gathering of frog-lovers without me present? Who is the leader of the Worldwide Fair Play for Frogs Committee and all its miscellaneous splinter groups if not me, Nestle J. Frobish? Who else, like a plumed knight, has cast his shining lance full and fair against the loathsome visage of every foe of frogs across the globe, and under every star in the whole heavens? Me, Nestle J. Frobish.

Sophistry will get you nowhere, Waldie. Only repentance for past sins and dedication to Truth, Beauty, and Fair Plays for Frogs. When you are ready to be shriven, I am ready to oblige.

Yours,

Nestle J. Frobish

Nestle J. Frobish

P.S. When you consult Freud and those psychiatrists, don't forget to inquire about your own frog-murder fixation.

JEROME R. WALDIE
MEMBER OF CONGRESS
14TH DISTRICT, CALIFORNIA

WASHINGTON ADDRESS:
Room 408
CANNON HOUSE OFFICE BUILDING
WASHINGTON, D.C. 20515
PHONE: 225-5511
AREA CODE: 202

COMMITTEES:
JUDICIARY
POST OFFICE AND CIVIL SERVICE
SELECT COMMITTEE ON CRIME

DISTRICT REPRESENTATIVE:
E. A. "PAT" FERGUSON
P.O. Box 864
Civic Center
CONCORD, CALIFORNIA 94520
PHONE: 687-1200
AREA CODE: 415

RICHMOND OFFICE:
3915 MACDONALD AVENUE
RICHMOND, CALIFORNIA 94805
PHONE: 233-4425

Congress of the United States
House of Representatives
Washington, D.C. 20515

August 13, 1970

Mr. Nestle J. Frobish
Lyndonville, Vermont 05851

Dear Mr. Frobish:

I had forgotten that Art Hoppe, a distinguished and disinterested chronicler of historical events, had recorded the auspicious event of my award from the frog-lovers.

That lapse, plus your compelling logic—and my overwhelming desire to be free of the plague to my conscience that you represent—cause me now to do as you suggest.

I repent. I dedicate myself to Truth, Beauty, and Fair Play for Frogs. I am ready to be shriven.

Sincerely yours,

Jerry Waldie

JEROME R. WALDIE
United States Congressman
Fourteenth District

JRW:mrr

San Francisco Chronicle

September 2, 1970

Dear Frobe:

Just think, after only ten years you have been victorious. I hope very much that you are not too exhausted to rededicate yourself to some new and equally worthy cause. How about razing the midi skirt?

Admiringly,

Art Hoppe

San Francisco, Calif. 94119

WORLDWIDE FAIRPLAY FOR FROGS COMMITTEE

MAIN OFFICE
LYNDONVILLE, VERMONT
* *
OVERSEAS OFFICE:
REDCOATS GREEN, ENGLAND

DISTRICT OFFICES:
BERKELEY, CALIF.
MARTINEZ, CALIF.
SANTA CRUZ, CALIF.
NEW HAVEN, CONN.
CAMBRIDGE, MASS.
AUSTIN, TEXAS
WASHINGTON, D.C.

August 20, 1970

Hon. Jerome Waldie
House Office Building
Washington, D. C. 20515

Dear Statesman Waldie:

My basic faith in the goodness of man, sorely tried by

FAIR PLAY FOR FROGS

you, has at last been vindicated. I am sure your peace of mind has noticeably improved since making this decision for frogs.

Since you are really the first Frog-Murderer ever to request shriving, I confess I am taken aback a little bit in applying the shrive, or whatever it is one does in this thing. For a moment I thought I might engage Mr. Sargent Shriver for the job, assuming he would know what to do, but he is occupied elsewhere.

I hope you will bear with me while I prepare a suitable procedure and ceremony for perfect absolution. In the meanwhile, you may consider yourself provisionally shriven, or shrived, or shrove, or whatever.

With deep respect for your emergent statesmanship and humanity, I am

Yours truly,

Nestle J. Frobish

Nestle J. Frobish

P.S.: While I am working this up, would you inquire to see if any of your colleagues have been harboring anti-frog tendencies? Perhaps we could have the shriving on a group plan.

JEROME R. WALDIE
MEMBER OF CONGRESS
14TH DISTRICT, CALIFORNIA

WASHINGTON ADDRESS:
Room 408
CANNON HOUSE OFFICE BUILDING
WASHINGTON, D.C. 20515
PHONE: 225-8811
AREA CODE: 202

COMMITTEES:
JUDICIARY
POST OFFICE AND CIVIL SERVICE
SELECT COMMITTEE ON CRIME

DISTRICT REPRESENTATIVE:
E. A. "PAT" FERGUSON
P.O. Box 864
CIVIC CENTER
CONCORD, CALIFORNIA 94520
PHONE: 687-1200
AREA CODE: 415

RICHMOND OFFICE:
3915 MACDONALD AVENUE
RICHMOND, CALIFORNIA 94805
PHONE: 233-4425

Congress of the United States
House of Representatives
Washington, D.C. 20515

September 11, 1970

Mr. Nestle J. Frobish
Lyndonville, Vermont 05851

Dear Mr. Frobish:

I am grateful for the provisional peace of mind you have extended me and will await anxiously the ultimate cleansing of such vestigial impurities in my character that still remain.

I hesitate to inquire of my colleagues as to any latent anti-frog tendencies they may possess, for fear that my mere inquiry may cause them to suspect the existence of that which I have thankfully renounced.

Sincerely yours,

JEROME R. WALDIE
United States Congressman
Fourteenth District

JRW:smo

WORLDWIDE FAIRPLAY FOR FROGS COMMITTEE

MAIN OFFICE
LYNDONVILLE, VERMONT
* *
OVERSEAS OFFICE
REDCOATS GREEN, ENGLAND

DISTRICT OFFICES
BERKELEY, CALIF.
MARTINEZ, CALIF.
SANTA CRUZ, CALIF.
NEW HAVEN, CONN.
CAMBRIDGE, MASS.
AUSTIN, TEXAS
WASHINGTON, D.C.

Lyndonville, Vermont 05851
November 8, 1970

Hon. Jerome Waldie
House Office Building
Washington, D. C.

Dear fellow Ranaphile:

First of all, congratulations on your re-election, now that you have renounced your previous violent tendencies against frogs. Countless thousands of frog-lovers the nation over now look to you to organize a strong, effective pro-frog bloc in the House, where it is badly needed. You may scoff at this, Waldie, but a strong and uncompromising pro-frog stand may just be the vital ingredient you need to win the speakership, which has eluded your grasp for so long.

You may be wondering why you have not been fully shriven on a permanent basis by now. The reason is that preparing the necessary legislation for you to introduce has been quite time-consuming. It is, however, under way. I know how anxious you must be to get on with this, but for the moment I can only send you the enclosed memento as an inspiration to you. I know you will want to place it prominently in your office, alongside Speaker

McCormack and President Nixon and Governor Reagan.
Onward and upward,

Nestle J. Frobish

Nestle J. Frobish
"Ned" to confirmed lovers of frogs
Enclosure: Outstanding frog picture

JEROME R. WALDIE
MEMBER OF CONGRESS
14TH DISTRICT, CALIFORNIA

WASHINGTON ADDRESS:
Room 408
Cannon House Office Building
Washington, D.C. 20515
Phone: 225-5511
Area Code: 202

COMMITTEES:
JUDICIARY
POST OFFICE AND CIVIL SERVICE
SELECT COMMITTEE ON CRIME

DISTRICT REPRESENTATIVE:
E. A. "Pat" Ferguson
P.O. Box 864
Civic Center
Concord, California 94520
Phone: 687-1200
Area Code: 415

Richmond Office:
3915 Macdonald Avenue
Richmond, California 94805
Phone: 233-4423

Congress of the United States
House of Representatives
Washington, D.C. 20515

January 4, 1971

Mr. Nestle J. Frobish
Worldwide Fair Play for Frogs Committee
Lyndonville, Vermont 05851

Dear Mr. Frobish:

The magnificent photo of a frog is placed, as you suggest, next to those for whom I have a certain amount of
respect and admiration.

I am taken aback by your assigned reason for the delay

in my shriving. I do not recall any shriven condition re-
quiring the introduction of legislation.

By the way, the glass on my frog photo was shattered
when delivered. Can you replace it?

Sincerely yours,

Jerry Waldie

JEROME R. WALDIE
United States Congressman
Fourteenth District

JRW:sd

Lyndonville, Vermont 05851

January 20, 1971

Hon. Jerome R. Waldie
House Office Building
Washington, DC 20515

Dear Congressman:

I am shocked to learn that your magnificent frog photograph arrived with the glass shattered. This can mean
only one thing: there is a hidden frog-hater somewhere
in the postal service. You can help weed him out by asking the chairman of the House Post Office Committee to
demand that the Postmaster General call for a full investigation. In the meantime, I would suggest that you
consult the foreman of the House furniture shop about
replacing the glass. I am sure that any replacement I
might send from here would risk falling into the hands of
the same miscreant who smashed the last one.

The reason you do not recall the role of legislation in the
shriving process is that nobody has ever been shrove or

shrived or shriven or whatever it is before. You are not the usual run-of-the-pond converted frog-murderer. You occupy a high position of profit and trust, and thus have the opportunity to make a commensurate contribution to the welfare of frogdom. When I can get this omnibus bill ready, I know you will want to enlist the many others under your influence in the Congress to join you in introducing it. I can understand your restiveness, being only provisionally shriven and eager for full and permanent absolution, but I trust you will bear with me.

Rana semper vici,

Nestle Frobish

WORLDWIDE FAIRPLAY FOR FROGS COMMITTEE

MAIN OFFICE
LYNDONVILLE, VERMONT
* *
OVERSEAS OFFICE:
REDCOATS GREEN, ENGLAND

DISTRICT OFFICES:
BERKELEY, CALIF.
MARTINEZ, CALIF.
SANTA CRUZ, CALIF.
NEW HAVEN, CONN.
CAMBRIDGE, MASS.
AUSTIN, TEXAS
WASHINGTON, D.C.

Lyndonville, Vt. 05851
March 15, 1971

Honorable Jerome Waldie
House Office Building
Washington, D. C.

Dear Congressman Waldie:
Great news! After assiduous research, and the assistance of a team of dedicated lawyers, I have at last assembled the Omnibus Frog Protection Act of 1971 that you have

FAIR PLAY FOR FROGS

been waiting so anxiously to introduce. Its introduction will complete your shriving as a reformed frog murderer–fellow traveler.

Enclosed you will find the bill, ready for introduction; a section-by-section analysis; and a draft of your remarks for the special order.

Naturally, your modesty will probably prevent you from soliciting the support of other influential members of the House, so I have taken the liberty of preparing some draft remarks for several of them also. These have been forwarded directly to them; copies are enclosed. I chose three from each party to emphasize the bipartisan nature of this bill.

The bill is probably self-explanatory, but you may wonder why I specified that National Frog Week shall be the week in which January 9 occurs. That happens to be President Nixon's birthday, and I chose it for National Frog Week mainly to protect against a possible veto. I may not be an expert in politics, but I know a thing or two.

Please rush me ten thousand reprints of the special order from the *Congressional Record*. I assume you will send out several hundred thousand copies with the frank, as well, to those who undoubtedly receive your baby books, menu books, and farmers' yearbooks, etc.

Enthusiastically,

Nestle J. Frobish

Nestle J. Frobish
President

FAIR PLAY FOR FROGS

_____ CONGRESS

_____ Session

H.R. _____

Grorge R Waldie

(Original signature of Member)

IN THE HOUSE OF REPRESENTATIVES

Mr. **WALDIE** _____ introduced the following bill; which was referred

to the Committee on _____

A BILL

(Insert title of bill here)

To protect the humble frog

SEC. 1. Short Title

Be it enacted by the Senate and House of Representatives of the United States of America in Congress assembled, that this act may be cited as the "Omnibus Frog Protection Act of 1971."

SEC. 2. Declaration of Policy

The Congress finds that since the first settlement of North America the humble frog, genus Rana, has been an important part of America; that over the years the public has lost sight of the contributions of the frog to the American way of life; that thoughtless and malicious persons have from time to time chosen to oppress the humble frog, either for commercial gain or from various forms of inner depravity; that such activities have worked

FAIR PLAY FOR FROGS

a serious hardship on the frogs of America, interfering with their rights to life, liberty, and the pursuit of happiness; that a major priority of the decade of the seventies must be to rectify this situation; and that in enacting this act Congress intends to show the American people that it does not aim to play second fiddle to anybody in achieving this objective.

SEC. 3. Game and Bird Preserves
        Section 683 of Title 16, U. S. C., is amended to read as follows:
        "§683. Areas set aside for protection of game, fish, and frogs; unlawfully taking game, fish *or frogs.*

The President of the United States is authorized to designate such areas on any lands which have been, or which may hereafter be, purchased by the United States under the provisions of sections 480, 500, 513–519, and 521 of this title, and Acts supplementary thereto and amendatory thereof, as should in his opinion, be set aside for the protection of game animals, birds, fish, *or frogs;* and, except under such rules and regulations as the Secretary of Agriculture may from time to time prescribe, it shall be unlawful for any person to hunt, catch, trap, willfully disturb or kill any kind of game animal, game or nongame birds, fish, *or frog,* or take the eggs of any such bird on any lands so set aside, or in or on the waters thereof."

SEC. 4. Fish, Game, and Frog Sanctuaries in National Forests
        (a) Section 694 of Title 16, U. S. C., is amended to read as follows:
        "§694. Fish, game *and frog* sanctuaries in national forests; establishment by President.

FAIR PLAY FOR FROGS

For the purpose of providing breeding places for game birds, game animals, fish *and frogs* on lands and waters in the national forests not chiefly suitable for agriculture, the President of the United States is authorized, upon recommendation of the Secretary of Agriculture and the Secretary of Commerce and with the approval of the State legislatures of the respective States in which said national forests are situated, to establish by public proclamation certain specified and limited areas within said forests as fish and game sanctuaries or refuges which shall be devoted to the increase of game birds, game animals, fish, *and frogs* of all kinds naturally adapted thereto, but it is not intended that the lands included in such fish and game sanctuaries or refuges shall cease to be parts of the national forests wherein they are located, and the establishment of such fish and game sanctuaries or refuges shall not prevent the Secretary of Agriculture from permitting other uses of the national forests under and in conformity with the laws and the rules and regulations applicable thereto so far as such uses may be consistent with the purposes for which such fish and game sanctuaries or refuges are authorized to be established."

(b) Section 694a of Title 16, U. S. C., is amended to read as follows:

"§694a. Same; hunting, pursuing, capturing, etc., unlawful.

When such fish and game sanctuaries or refuges have been established as provided in section 694 of this title, hunting, pursuing, poisoning, angling for, killing, or capturing by trapping, netting, or any other means, or attempting to hunt, pursue, angle for, kill, or capture

FAIR PLAY FOR FROGS

any wild animals, fish, *or frogs* for any purpose whatever upon the lands of the United States within the limits of said fish and game sanctuaries or refuges shall be unlawful except as hereinafter provided."

SEC. 5. Wildlife Refuges; Penalties
Section 41 of Title 18, U. S. C. is amended to read as follows:
"§41. Hunting, fishing, trapping; disturbance or injury on wildlife refuges.

Whoever, except in compliance with rules and regulations promulgated by authority of law, hunts, traps, captures, willfully disturbs or kills any bird, fish, *frog* or wild animal of any kind whatever, or takes or destroys the eggs or nest of any such bird, fish, *or frog,* on any lands or waters which are set apart or reserved as sanctuaries, refuges or breeding grounds for such birds, fish, *frogs,* or animals under any law of the United States or willfully injures, molests, or destroys any property of the United States on such lands or waters, shall be fined not more than $500 or imprisoned not more than six months, or both."

SEC. 6. Hunting Frogs from Aircraft and Motor Vehicles Prohibited
The catch line and subsection (a) of Section 47 of Title 18, U. S. C., are amended to read as follows:
"§47. Use of aircraft or motor vehicles to hunt certain wild horses, burros, *or frogs;* pollution of watering holes.

(a) Whoever uses an aircraft or a motor vehicle to hunt, for the purpose of capturing or killing, any wild unbranded horse, mare, colt or burro running at large on any of the public land or ranges, *or any frog inhabiting such land or ranges,* shall be fined not more than $500, or imprisoned not more than six months, or both."

Sec. 7. Devices for Taking Frogs; Transportation Forbidden
Section 48 of Title 18, U. S. C., is added to read as follows:
"§48. Devices for taking frogs; transportation forbidden in interstate and foreign commerce.

Whoever knowingly transports in interstate commerce or from any foreign country into the United States any article, instrument, trap or device specifically designed and intended for the taking of frogs shall be fined not more than $1000 or imprisoned not more than one year, or both."

Sec. 8. Devices for Taking Frogs Nonmailable
The first paragraph of section 1716 of Title 18, U. S. C., is amended to read as follows:
"§1716. Injurious articles considered nonmailable.

All kinds of poison, and all articles and compositions containing poison, and all poisonous animals, insects, reptiles, and all explosives, inflammable materials, infernal machines, and mechanical, chemical, or other devices or compositions which may ignite or explode, and all disease germs or scabs, and all other natural or artificial articles, compositions, or material which may kill or injure another, or injure the mails or other property, *and all articles, instruments, traps or devices specifically designed and intended for the taking of frogs,* whether or not sealed as first class matter, are nonmailable matter and shall not be conveyed in the mails or delivered from any post office or station thereof, nor by any letter carrier."

FAIR PLAY FOR FROGS

SEC. 9. National Frog Week

Section 156A of Title 36, U. S. C., is added to read as follows:

"§156A. National Frog Week.

The President is authorized and requested to issue annually a proclamation designating the week in which January 9 occurs as National Frog Week, and calling upon all citizens during such week to pay tributes to the humble frog whose presence during the past four centuries has so enriched the lives of Americans of every race, creed and color."

SEC. 10. National Fair Play for Frogs Committee, Inc.

Chapter 41A of Title 36, U. S. C., is added to read as follows:

"CHAPTER 41A NATIONAL FAIR PLAY FOR FROGS COMMITTEE, INC.

Sec.

1061 Corporation created.
1062 Completion of organization.
1063 Purposes of corporation.
1064 Powers of corporation.
1065 Membership.
1066 Governing body; meetings.
1067 Officers of corporation; selection; tenure; duties.
1068 Principal office; resident agent.
1069 Distribution of income or assets to members; loans.
1070 Nonpolitical nature of corporation.
1071 Liability for acts of officers and agents.
1072 Prohibition against issuance of stock or payment of dividends.
1073 Books and records; inspection.
1074 Report to Congress on activities.

§1061. Corporation Created.

The following persons, to wit: Nestle J. Frobish of Lyndonville, Vermont, Jerome Waldie of Antioch, California, and Arthur Hoppe of San Francisco, California; are created and declared to be a body corporate of the District of Columbia, where its legal domicile shall be, by the name of the National Fair Play for Frogs Committee, Inc. (hereinafter referred to as the corporation), and by such name shall be known and have perpetual succession and the powers limitations and restrictions herein contained. It shall be the duty of the persons named in this section, jointly and severally, to file with the Superintendent of Corporations of the District of Columbia a copy of this chapter within fifteen days after December 31, 1971.

§1062. Completion of organization.

A majority of the persons named in section 1061 of this title acting in person or by written proxy, are authorized to complete the organization of the corporation by the selection of officers and employees, the adoption of a constitution and bylaws not inconsistent with this chapter, and the doing of such other acts as may be necessary for such purpose.

§1063. Purposes of Corporation.

The purposes of the corporation shall be: to educate the public in the contributions made by the humble frog throughout American history; to speak out against all forms of oppression and tyranny over the humble frog; and everywhere, in all respects to work for the interests of the frogs of the United States, all the while maintaining true allegiance to the government of the United States, protecting her from all enemies domestic and foreign, and participating in activities demonstrating patriotism, public spirit and devotion to the highest ideals as will create additional public respect and support for the corporation and its objectives.

§1064. Powers of Corporation.

The corporation shall have power—

(1) to have succession by its corporate name;

(2) to sue and be sued, complain and defend in any court of competent jurisdiction;

(3) to adopt, use, and alter a corporate seal;

(4) to choose such officers, managers, agents, and employees as the activities of the corporation may require;

(5) to adopt, amend and alter a constitution and bylaws; not inconsistent with the laws of the United States or of any State in which the corporation is to operate, for the management of its property and the regulation of its affairs;

(6) to contract and be contracted with;

(7) to take by lease, gift, purchase, grant, devise, or bequest from any public body or agency or any private corporation, association, partnership, firm, or individual and to hold absolutely or in trust for any of the purposes of the corporation any property real, personal, or mixed, necessary or convenient for attaining the objects and carrying into effect the purposes of the corporation, subject, however, to applicable provisions of law of any State (A) governing the amount of or kind of property which may be held by, or (B) otherwise limiting or controlling the ownership of property by, a corporation operating in such State;

(8) to transfer, convey, lease, sublease, mortgage, encumber and otherwise alienate real, personal, or mixed property; and

(9) to borrow money for the purpose of the corporation, issue bonds therefor, and secure the same by mortgage, deed of trust, pledge, or otherwise, subject in every case to all applicable provisions of Federal and State laws; and

(10) to do any and all acts and things necessary and proper to carry out the objects and purposes of the corporation.

§1065. Membership.

Membership in the corporation shall be open to all residents of the United States who have subscribed to the purposes of the corporation and who continue to exhibit their devotion to those purposes in their daily lives.

§1066. Governing body; meetings.

The supreme governing authority of the corporation shall be the national convention thereof, composed of such officers and elected representatives from the several States and other local subdivisions of the corporate organization as shall be provided by the constitution and bylaws. The meetings of the national convention may be held in any State or Territory or in the District of Columbia.

§1067. Officers of corporation; selection; tenure; duties.

The officers of the corporation shall be selected in such a manner and for such terms and with such duties and titles as may be prescribed in the constitution and bylaws of the corporation.

§1068. Principal office; resident agent.

The principal office of the corporation shall be located in the State of Vermont, but the corporation shall have in the District at all times a designated agent authorized to accept service of process, notice, or demand for the corporation, and service of such process, notice, or demand required or permitted by law to be served upon the corporation may be served upon such agent. The corporation shall file with the Superintendent of Corporations of the District of Columbia a statement designating the initial and each successor registered agent of the corporation and the initial and each successor registered office of the corporation immediately following any such designation. As used in this chapter the term "Superintendent of Corporations of the District of Columbia" means the Commissioners of the District of Columbia or any agent designated by them to perform the functions vested by this chapter in the Superintendent of Corporations.

§1069. Distribution of income or assets to members; loans.

(a) No part of the income or assets of the corporation shall inure to any of its members or officers as such, or be distributable to any of them during the life of the corporation or upon its dissolution or final liquidation. Nothing in this subsection, however, shall be construed to prevent the payment of compensation to officers of the corporation or reimbursement for actual necessary expenses in amounts approved by the council of administration of the corporation.

(b) The corporation shall not make loans to its officers or employees. Any member of the council of administration who votes for or assents to the making of a loan or advance to any officer or employee of the corporation, and any officers who participate in the making of such loan or advance, shall be jointly and severally liable to the corporation for the amount of such loan until the repayment thereof.

§1070. Nonpolitical nature of corporation.

The corporation and its officers and agents as such shall not contribute to any political party or candidate for public office.

§1071. Liability for acts of officers and agents.

The corporation shall be liable for the acts of its officers and agents when acting within the scope of their authority.

§1072. Prohibition against issuance of stock or payment of dividends.

The corporation shall have no power to issue any shares of stock or to declare or pay any dividends.

§1073. Books and records; inspection.

The corporation shall keep correct and complete books and records of account and shall keep minutes of the proceedings of its national conventions and council of administration. All books and records of the corporation may be inspected by any member, or his agent or attorney, for any proper purpose, at any reasonable time.

§1074. Report to Congress on Activities.

On or before March 1 of each year the President of the corporation shall report to the Congress on its activities during the preceding year at a joint session of Congress duly assembled.

§1075. Exclusive right to name, emblems, seals and badges.

FAIR PLAY FOR FROGS

The corporation shall have the sole and exclusive right to use the name "National Fair Play for Frogs Committee, Inc.," and no other organization shall use the name "National Fair Play for Frogs Committee, Inc." The corporation shall have the exclusive and sole right to use, or to allow or refuse the use of, such emblems, seals and badges as may hereafter be designed and adopted by the corporation.

§1076. Use of assets on dissolution or liquidation.

Upon dissolution or final liquidation of the corporation, after discharge or satisfaction of all outstanding obligations and liabilities, the remaining assets, if any, of the corporation shall be distributed in accordance with the determination of the national executive board and in compliance with the constitution and bylaws of the corporation and all Federal and State laws applicable thereto.

§1077. Reservation or right to amend or repeal chapter.

The right to alter, amend, or repeal this chapter is expressly reserved.

THE OMNIBUS FROG PROTECTION ACT OF 1971

Section by Section Analysis

Sec. 1 Short Title: "Omnibus Frog Protection Act of 1971"

Sec. 2 Declaration of Policy

Congress finds that the humble frog has made an important contribution to American life and states that the protection of the frog shall be a major priority of the nineteen seventies.

Sec. 3 Game and Bird Preserves

This section authorizes the President to establish preserves for the protection of frogs as well as for game animals, birds, and fish.

Sec. 4 Fish, game and frog sanctuaries in national forests

This section authorizes the President to proclaim areas within national forests as protected breeding places for frogs as well as for game birds, game animals and fish.

Sec. 5 Wildlife refuges: penalties

This section provides a penalty of $500, or six months imprisonment, or both, for persons who hunt, trap or disturb frogs in designated sanctuaries, refuges or breeding grounds.

Sec. 6 Hunting Frogs from Aircraft and Motor Vehicles Prohibited

This section prohibits the hunting of frogs from aircraft or motor vehicles and provides a fine of $500, or imprisonment for six months, or both, as a penalty.

Sec. 7 Devices for taking frogs: transportation forbidden

This section prohibits the transportation in interstate or foreign commerce of any article, instrument, trap or device specifically designed and intended for the taking of frogs, and provides a penalty of not more than $1000, or one year imprisonment, or both.

Sec. 8 Devices for taking frogs nonmailable

This section prohibits the sending through the U. S. mails of articles specifically designed and intended for the taking of frogs.

Sec. 9 National Frog Week

This section authorizes and requests the President to proclaim the week in which January 9 occurs as National Frog Week, calling upon all citizens to pay tribute to the frog during such week.

Sec. 10 National Fair Play for Frogs Committee: charter

This section incorporates the National Fair Play for Frogs Committee, Inc. as a congressionally chartered, nonprofit organization dedicated to protecting and honoring the humble frog, and for other patriotic purposes.

DRAFT REMARKS OF MR. WALDIE ON INTRODUCTION OF THE OMNIBUS FROG PROTECTION ACT OF 1971 (SPECIAL ORDER)

MR. WALDIE: Mr. Speaker, I rise today to introduce what can only be described as an historic piece of legislation, the Omnibus Frog Protection Act of 1971.

The humble frog has been a sadly neglected part of our American way of life.

When the Pilgrims stepped ashore at Plymouth Rock, they were greeted by the amiable croak of the frog, crouching in his aqueous lair, welcoming their brother creatures to a new world.

When the colonists of Jamestown battled to launch their little settlement against the perils of disease, starvation, and hostile savages, the humble frog stood beside them in those Virginia swamps, bellowing out his cry of encouragement and support.

And I am sure, Mr. Speaker, that had it not been winter at Valley Forge, General Washington's army too would have delighted in the inspiration provided by the patriotic frogs of Pennsylvania.

FAIR PLAY FOR FROGS

But despite this early and frequent association with the great events of our history, we Americans have all too often neglected the humble frog. If this continues, Mr. Speaker, it may someday be too late. We may awake to discover that the humble frog is no longer with us, having been ruthlessly extirpated by the murderers of frogs who, notwithstanding the general progress of mankind from barbarism to civilization, still abound.

I did not always recognize this fact, Mr. Speaker. Ten years ago, before I came to this body, I served as an assemblyman in my native state of California. In the course of my diligent duties there I caused to be introduced a wicked, evil bill.

It was a bill—and it pains me even now to relate this— that authorized the taking of frogs by slingshot in the state of California.

Since that occasion, night after sleepless night I wondered why I had done such a thing. Why had I yielded to the blandishments of the frog murderers who, I am sorry to say, inhabited the low lying areas of my assembly district? I wondered even more when, on the occasion of my next election campaign, my treasurer noted that not a nickel of contributions had arrived from the frog murderers of my district, despite his repeated appeals. In retrospect, this fact, as much as any other, brings home to me the perfidy and iniquity of persons who prey on frogs.

Yet I had not in my own mind felt guilty about my unconscionable act, perhaps because the Assembly Fish and Game Committee, composed of solons wiser than I, disposed of my bill without a trace. But then a chain of events began which culminated in my complete conversion, and for that I am eternally grateful to a remarkable citizen and patriot, the nation's foremost friend of frogs,

FAIR PLAY FOR FROGS

that unsung foe of tyranny, that Champion of Right, Mr. Nestle J. Frobish, now of Lyndonville, Vermont.

Certainly I had earned the opprobrium and revulsion of all decent people by sponsoring this iniquitous bill, and only a truly great man would have devoted his best efforts of a decade to helping me see the error of my ways. Mr. Frobish is such a man.

Today, Mr. Speaker, thanks to the relentless logic and persistent efforts of Mr. Frobish, I am shriven of my past sins. I am today a friend of frogs, as is he. My past is redeemed, and my salvation is assured, at least with respect to that particular transgression.

In 1961 Mr. Frobish singlehandedly, in the face of enormous public indifference and a complete news blackout, formed the Fair Play for Frogs Committee. Its sole cause for the past ten years, Mr. Speaker, so far as I can determine, has been setting me straight about the importance and intrinsic worth of the humble frog.

Today my introduction of this historic legislation constitutes the final act of my shriving. My sin is gone, and I look forward to many years of personal crusading on behalf of frogs with a redeemed conscience, at last.

I could continue at some length, Mr. Speaker, on the virtues of Mr. Frobish, but in view of his modest and retiring nature it would be inappropriate of me to do so, beyond extending to him my deepest and most heartfelt gratitude.

Turning now to the provisions of the bill, I should first point out that there is one small item on the books already which can, if attentively administered, serve to protect the humble frog. This is the Federal Endangered Species Conservation Act of 1969. Under this act the Secretary of the Interior may take action to protect endangered species of animals, including amphibians. This gives the government a powerful weapon on the frog's behalf, if at any time, God forbid, his numbers should drop to the danger point.

Passage of the Omnibus Frog Protection Act, however, will make it unlikely that this grave situation will occur. Section 1 contains the short title of the bill.

Section 2 contains the Congressional policy, which I quote in full:

"The Congress finds that since the first settlement of North America the humble frog, genus Rana, has been an important part of America; that over the years the public has lost sight of the contributions of the frog to the American way of life; that thoughtless and malicious persons have from time to time chosen to oppress the humble frog, either for commercial gain or from various forms of inner depravity; that such activities have worked a serious hardship on the frogs of America, interfering with their rights to life, liberty, and the pursuit of happiness; that a major priority of the decade of the seventies must be to rectify this situation; and that in enacting this act Congress intends to show the American people that it does not aim to play second fiddle to anybody in achieving this objective."

Section 3 amends existing law to provide that the President may establish preserves for the protection of frogs as well as for game animals, birds, and fish.

Section 4 authorizes the President to proclaim areas in national forests as protected breeding places for frogs as well as for game birds, game animals, and fish.

Section 5 provides a penalty of $500, or six months imprisonment, or both, for persons who hunt, trap, or disturb frogs in designated sanctuaries or breeding grounds.

Section 6 outlaws the hunting of frogs from aircraft

FAIR PLAY FOR FROGS

and motor vehicles, and provides a fine of $500, or six months imprisonment, or both. Admittedly we have little evidence of people hunting frogs from airplanes, but we enacted a similar provision to protect wild horses and burros just barely in time to prevent their extermination, and I see no point in letting things go too far before acting to protect the frog in the same way.

Section 7 prohibits the transportation of gigs and other frog-taking devices in interstate commerce, and provides a fine of $1000, one year imprisonment, or both for violators. As many members may know, the gig is an awful weapon. Snickety-snack, snickety-snack it goes, and the poor frog is lost.

Section 7 says no more of this barbarism.

Section 8 similarly outlaws the sending of gigs and other anti-frog devices through the U. S. mails.

Section 9 authorizes the President to proclaim National Frog Week, which is declared to be the week in which January 9 occurs. This proclamation will call the attention of citizens to the role of the frog, and thus build public approbation for this little-appreciated amphibian.

Section 10 adds a new chapter to Title 36 of the U. S. Code, incorporating the National Fair Play for Frogs Committee, Inc., along the lines of the Blue Star Mothers of America, the Jewish War Veterans, and other groups similarly favored by Congress. I am proud to be named in this section along with Mr. Frobish and that incomparable columnist, Mr. Arthur Hoppe of the San Francisco *Chronicle*, as the incorporators of this new organization. This charter also provides that Mr. Frobish, who will be the organization's first president, shall make a personal report each year to a joint session of Congress on the activities of the Committee. Too often Congress loses interest in corporations it charters; this provision ensures that the Committee's work will be described in detail to the Congress in a personal message from its president once a year. In this way Congress could profitably use the first six weeks of each session, now used only for getting acquainted.

Mr. Speaker, that concludes my description of the Omnibus Frog Protection Act of 1971. It is not a complicated bill, yet its implications are vital. It means that at last Congress recognizes and appreciates the role of the humble frog in American life, and declares that the protection of the frog shall henceforth be a pillar of national policy.

(Applause, members rising.)

MR. WALDIE (continuing): I now yield for tributes from my colleagues.

DRAFT REMARKS OF REP. CARL ALBERT ON INTRODUCTION
OF THE OMNIBUS FROG PROTECTION ACT OF 1971

MR. ALBERT (descending from the Chair): The gentleman from California (MR. WALDIE), who has so often been an inspiration to the leadership of this body, has once again performed an invaluable public service in introducing the Omnibus Frog Protection Act of 1971.

In his able address, the member from California has stated with his usual force and clarity the need for action now by this Congress to protect the humble frog. I can add nothing in logic or eloquence to those remarks.

It is significant that this bill is brought forward not by an ordinary member of this house, but by a man who has been a self-styled candidate for its highest office, the one I now happen to hold. Had he brought forth this landmark legislation two years ago, prior to his contest with former Speaker McCormack, who knows but what public

FAIR PLAY FOR FROGS

approbation and acclaim might have influenced the two hundred or so members who did not support him to switch their allegiance? But it is idle to speculate over great turning points of years past. What we must do now is protect the humble frog, and our esteemed colleague from California is once again leading the way.

DRAFT REMARKS OF REP. HALE BOGGS ON INTRODUCTION OF THE OMNIBUS FROG PROTECTION ACT OF 1971

MR. BOGGS: Mr. Speaker, I rise to congratulate the gentleman from California (MR. WALDIE) on his introduction of this important and much-needed legislation.

It is a little-known fact—if I may inject a personal note—but the name of the Boggs family actually stems from the penchant of my distant ancestors for dwelling in the lowland bogs of old England. There, amidst the rushes and the hummocks, the early Boggses undoubtedly paused often to appreciate the amiable croak of the humble frog.

It is significant, too, Mr. Speaker, that when the Boggses came to America, they quickly found their way to the bogs and bayous of the great state of Louisiana, the picturesque scenery, exotic wildlife, and oil of which they have assiduously protected ever since.

I am sure my ancestors, many of whom have by now no doubt turned into peat moss, would be highly pleased at my support of this bill.

DRAFT REMARKS OF REP. GERALD R. FORD ON INTRODUCTION OF THE OMNIBUS FROG PROTECTION ACT OF 1971

MR. GERALD R. FORD: Mr. Speaker, it is with great pleasure that I rise today to announce my support of the Omnibus

FAIR PLAY FOR FROGS

Frog Protection Act of 1971, and to commend its author, the gentleman from California (MR. WALDIE).

I have just come from a top-level meeting at the White House where the President briefed the Republican leadership on additional aspects of his 1971 domestic program, the mightiest and most determined instrument ever forged to cure the ills of American society, so many of which arose during the first eight years of the last decade under the Presidential regimes of the other party.

I am authorized to state at this time that the President has given me his personal assurance that funds returned to the States and local governments under his historic revenue-sharing plan, now before this body, may be used for locally designed programs for the protection of the humble frog. The President wants to make it perfectly clear that any such program for the protection of frogs will be free from encumbering Federal interference.

So, Mr. Speaker, I say let us get on with the important business of this House. Let us pass these great acts now before us. Let us adopt the President's program, and let us also, in the spirit of bipartisan reconciliation, adopt the Omnibus Frog Protection Act authored by the member from California, so esteemed in the councils of his party.

DRAFT REMARKS OF REP. H. R. GROSS ON
INTRODUCTION OF THE OMNIBUS FROG PROTECTION
ACT OF 1971

MR. GROSS: Mr. Speaker, I have been a member of this body for twenty-two years, and during that time I have never discovered a bill that made any sense, or conserved the taxpayers' money, or reduced the empires of grasping bureaucrats, or simply any bill that I liked.

Now I can say that no more. I like this bill. I would

FAIR PLAY FOR FROGS

extol it at greater length, but mindful that the taxpayer must pay for the printing of the Record, I will desist.

DRAFT REMARKS OF REP. JAMES O'HARA ON INTRODUCTION OF THE OMNIBUS FROG PROTECTION ACT OF 1971

MR. O'HARA: Mr. Speaker, the gentleman from California (MR. WALDIE), whom I am proud to include among the left-leaning members of this house, has once again blazed the trail for us to follow.

His Omnibus Frog Protection Act, introduced today, is of course only a small first step, but it offers a sound foundation on which to build.

Concurrent with the introduction of this bill, the Democratic Study Group is forming a task force to plan for the further protection of the humble frog. As usual, we have no shortage of sound and badly needed solutions to the problems of the frog, which today constitute a national shame and disgrace.

We may propose a National Frog Protection Administration, with powers to take land by eminent domain, flood it, and convert it into frog refuges. This would be financed by Treasury borrowing, and the repayments would go into a revolving fund for further use, so that the gentleman from Texas (MR. MAHON) and his Committee cannot obstruct progress.

We may propose a massive new public works program whereby thousands of Americans thrown out of work by the President's economic policies can be gainfully employed constructing swamps for the humble frog. We may even come forward with a Marshall Plan for Frogs, in collaboration with the Junior Senator from Minnesota

FAIR PLAY FOR FROGS

(MR. HUMPHREY). Who, in fact, knows what we will do?

This is a great day, Mr. Speaker, but stick around, because there is scarcely any proposal that our Democratic Study Group cannot amplify into a major national commitment.

DRAFT REMARKS OF REP. JOHN ASHBROOK ON INTRODUCTION OF THE OMNIBUS FROG PROTECTION ACT OF 1971

MR. ASHBROOK: Mr. Speaker, I rise to join with my colleagues in praising the Frog Protection Act of 1971.

It may be said that protecting frogs is a radical-liberal issue.

It may be said that the use of Federal power for this purpose exceeds the powers granted to the Federal government under the Constitution.

It may be said that this act represents the entering wedge of the insidious international communist conspiracy.

I deny it, Mr. Speaker.

And if I deny it, Mr. Speaker, who will dare say that I am mistaken? After all, if anybody in the house can spot the entering wedge of international communism, it is the gentleman from Ohio (MR. ASHBROOK). Or perhaps the gentleman from Louisiana (MR. RARICK). Just to be on the safe side, I have checked with the gentleman from Louisiana and can report that he can find no traces of communism in this bill either.

So I say to you, this is an American bill. This is a bill worthy of a great nation, whose patriotic sons have for seven generations given their lives to stem the tide of various un-American movements, and who are even now helping our trusty yellow brothers of the Republic of South Viet Nam to lop off yet one more arm of the communist octopus in the far off jungles of Laos.

It must pass, Mr. Speaker. As for most of the other things pending before this body, however, I remain staunchly opposed.

WORLDWIDE FAIRPLAY FOR FROGS COMMITTEE

MAIN OFFICE
LYNDONVILLE, VERMONT
• •
OVERSEAS OFFICE:
REDCOATS GREEN, ENGLAND

DISTRICT OFFICES:
BERKELEY, CALIF.
MARTINEZ, CALIF.
SANTA CRUZ, CALIF.
NEW HAVEN, CONN.
CAMBRIDGE, MASS.
AUSTIN, TEXAS
WASHINGTON, D.C.

Lyndonville, Vt. 05851
March 15, 1971

Mr. Arthur Hoppe
Ace Newsman
San Francisco Chronicle
San Francisco, California

Dear Art:

I think the self-explanatory materials enclosed are sufficiently self-explanatory that I won't have to explain them.

I knew you would want to be the first to know about this, since you have kept the whole at times ugly story before the public during these ten trying years. This will be a great scoop for you, Art. It may make you famous. Along with me, of course, and Congressman Waldie, that body's foremost friend of frogs.

Be sure to rush me copies of the whole spread when it hits.

Yours for the humble frog,

Nestle J. Frobish

Nestle J. Frobish

ARTHUR HOPPE
April 1st, 1971

Dear Nestle:
I'm thinking.
Admiringly yours,

Arthur Hoppe

Arthur Hoppe
San Francisco Chronicle/San Francisco/California

WORLDWIDE FAIRPLAY FOR FROGS COMMITTEE

MAIN OFFICE
LYNDONVILLE, VERMONT
*   *
OVERSEAS OFFICE:
REDCOATS GREEN, ENGLAND

DISTRICT OFFICES:
BERKELEY, CALIF.
MARTINEZ, CALIF.
SANTA CRUZ, CALIF.
NEW HAVEN, CONN.
CAMBRIDGE, MASS.
AUSTIN, TEXAS
WASHINGTON, D.C.

Lyndonville, Vermont 05851
April 2, 1971

Hon. Jerome Waldie
House Office Building
Washington, D. C.

Dear Fellow Friend of Frogs:
I have watched anxiously for the introduction of the Omnibus Frog Protection Act by you, and am frankly

FAIR PLAY FOR FROGS

getting a little nervous. I know how eager you have been for final shriving of your past sins, and thus your failure to take this historic step immediately puzzles me. Please advise as to the cause of the delay. If you need a little last minute reinforcement, I will gladly send along some stirring exhortations on the importance of preserving the humble frog, culled from my noted works of the last decade.

March 21 has come and gone. Of that there can be no doubt. That was, of course, the Tenth Anniversary of the introduction of your notorious Frog-Murder Bill in the California assembly. I know you greeted that solemn date with a clean conscience at last, having been provisionally shrived, and rapidly approaching the day of final atonement.

I am presently organizing the Worldwide Frog-Lovers March on Washington in support of you and your landmark bill. Would you be good enough to ask the National Capital Park Service if it is all right if about 500,000 people camp out along the Anacostia, in the general vicinity of Karl Hess's houseboat? We will also want an audience with the President, which I trust you will arrange for us at your weekly meetings with him. Please let me know what date would be best to give you maximum exposure at this event. We are, of course, a nonpartisan organization, but we are not above providing a forum through which illustrious Friends of Frogs can advance their own aspirations to higher office.

Expectantly,

Nestle J. Frobish

Nestle J. Frobish

WORLDWIDE FAIRPLAY FOR FROGS
COMMITTEE

MAIN OFFICE:
LYNDONVILLE, VERMONT
•   •
OVERSEAS OFFICE:
REDCOATS GREEN, ENGLAND

DISTRICT OFFICES:
BERKELEY, CALIF.
MARTINEZ, CALIF.
SANTA CRUZ, CALIF.
NEW HAVEN, CONN.
CAMBRIDGE, MASS.
AUSTIN, TEXAS
WASHINGTON, D.C.

Lyndonville, Vt. 05851
April 5, 1971

Mr. Art Hoppe
San Francisco Chronicle
San Francisco, California 94119

Dear Art:

Getting a letter from you, dated April 1st, announcing that you are "thinking," makes me suspicious.

I am also, frankly, getting very suspicious of my recent convert to the frog-lovers of the world, Mr. Waldie. I have been waiting patiently for two weeks for him to introduce the bill, but no action and not even any explanation.

I even wrote him last week, in high spirits, asking him to get Park Service approval for me and about 500,000 of my frog-loving friends to camp out along the Anacostia during our planned Frog-lover's March on Washington. So far no reply to that either.

I think you should call him directly, as an ace newsman, and probe his intentions. A probe for Frobe, you might call it.

Unless I get some action pretty damn quick, I am going

to expunge his provisional shriving and tell this whole filthy story to the world. Before you do.
Anxiously,

Nestle J. Frobish
P.S.: My work of a decade destroyed in a moment of perfidy! Think of it. While you are thinking.

April 6, 1971

Mr. Nestle J. Frobish
Worldwide Fair Play for Frogs Committee
Lyndonville, Vermont 05851

Dear Mr. Frobish:

Thank you for your recent letter of April 2, 1971.

I have submitted your most worthwhile legislative effort to various agencies and committee chairmen for comment and analysis.

This is somewhat time-consuming but necessary for success.

I recently came across the enclosed and wonder if the Committee could purchase one for me as an indication of their pride in my deigning to become a Member?

Sincerely yours,

JEROME R. WALDIE
United States Congressman
Fourteenth District

JRW:smo
Enclosure: ad for porcelain frog

WORLDWIDE FAIRPLAY FOR FROGS COMMITTEE

MAIN OFFICE
LYNDONVILLE, VERMONT
*   *
OVERSEAS OFFICE
REDCOATS GREEN, ENGLAND

DISTRICT OFFICES
BERKELEY, CALIF.
MARTINEZ, CALIF.
SANTA CRUZ, CALIF.
NEW HAVEN, CONN.
CAMBRIDGE, MASS.
AUSTIN, TEXAS
WASHINGTON, D.C.

Lyndonville, Vt. 05851
April 10, 1971

Hon. Jerome Waldie
House Office Building
Washington, D. C. 20515

Dear Congressman Waldie:

What you do not seem to understand is that there is a whole nation out there yearning to raise their voices in lusty crescendo on behalf of a Great Champion who will cast his shining lance full and fair in the face of the foes of Frogdom. So why are you fooling around? Introduce the bill, and I can absolutely promise you there will be a terrific reaction.

I should point out that this is not a pork-barrel bill like you are no doubt used to slipping through to put some freeway through Contra Costa County. This is a public interest issue. No need to make those sleazy deals with crusty old committee chairmen, most of whom, I am told, you do not approve of anyway. Put the bill in, and let public opinion force them to do your bidding!

In any case, if you must persist in this dilatory process—while the humble frog battles against extinction

FAIR PLAY FOR FROGS

every day—at least give me the names of the relevant committees and chairman so that I and the thousands of frog-lovers in their respective districts can get them straight on this vital issue.

We will be delighted to buy you the porcelain frog, as the leading advocate of fair play for frogs in the Congress. We can do this as soon as the bill goes through Congress, as the new §1064(7) of Title 36 USC, as added by Sec. 10 of your bill, takes effect. That is the section that allows the National Fair Play for Frogs Committee, Inc. to receive gifts which, following a favorable ruling on our 501(c) (3) request from IRS, will no doubt be forthcoming in amounts sufficient to cover the cost of the porcelain frog many times over. I can think of no more fitting tribute to the Man Who Got the Frog Bill Through Congress, as you will no doubt thereafter be fondly known.

Expectantly,

Nestle J. Frobish

Nestle J. Frobish

WORLDWIDE FAIRPLAY FOR FROGS COMMITTEE

MAIN OFFICE
LYNDONVILLE VERMONT

•

OVERSEAS OFFICE
REDCOATS GREEN, ENGLAND

DISTRICT OFFICES

BERKELEY, CALIF,
MARTINEZ, CALIF,
SANTA CRUZ, CALIF,
NEW HAVEN, CONN.
CAMBRIDGE, MASS.
AUSTIN, TEXAS
WASHINGTON, D.C.

Lyndonville, Vt. 05851

April 26, 1971

Honorable Paul N. McCloskey Jr.
House Office Building
Washington, D. C.

Dear Congressman McCloskey:

I am writing you because maybe you can help. Not me, but your traveling companion Mr. Jerome Waldie.

You see, Mr. Waldie has for years had a strange frog-murder fixation. Yes, astonishing as it may seem, Congressman Waldie wants to kill frogs—kill, kill, KILL. Frogs, of all creatures! Frogs, those benevolent friends of mankind who, crouching in their aqueous lair, seek only to enrich the lives of mankind with the pleasant chug-garum of a summer's evening!

This fixation first came out ten years ago, when then-assemblyman Waldie introduced the infamous Frog-Murder Bill in the California assembly. That was the bill, you may recall, which said "Frogs may be taken by using a slingshot." As chairman of the local Fair Play for Frogs Committee at that time, I remonstrated with Mr. Waldie. I kept on remonstrating, appealing to his better nature, if

FAIR PLAY FOR FROGS

any, for ten long years until, last fall, he agreed to repent his earlier sins and be shriven.

Never having shriven a Member of Congress before, or for that matter, anyone, I spent a lot of time and effort drafting the Omnibus Frog Protection Act of 1971 for him to introduce, along with several score of his colleagues. I even wrote all the floor speeches for Speaker Albert, Rep. Boggs, Rep. Ford, Rep. Ashbrook, Rep. Gross, and Rep. O'Hara. Alas, Mr. Waldie seems to have had a change of heart. He refuses to introduce the bill.

Since you traveled halfway around the globe with him, I am sure he has come to value your judgment. You will be doing him a favor by encouraging him now to renounce his past sins, sponsor this epochal measure to protect the humble frog, and lift the awful burden from his weary conscience.

Yours truly,

Nestle J. Frobish

Nestle J. Frobish
President

PAUL N. McCLOSKEY, JR.
11th District, California

COMMITTEE ON
GOVERNMENT OPERATIONS
AND
COMMITTEE ON
MERCHANT MARINE
AND FISHERIES

Congress of the United States
House of Representatives
Washington, D.C. 20515

May 11, 1971

Mr. Nestle J. Frobish, President
Worldwide Fair Play for Frogs Committee
Lyndonville, Vermont 05851

Dear Mr. Frobish:

I was pleased to receive your letter of April 26. I have a great deal of respect for Mr. Waldie, and it is difficult for me to understand his antagonistic position on your frog bill.

You will be glad to know that as we passed through Saigon last month, Mr. Waldie showed me a photograph he had taken from one of the Saigon newspapers showing the .picture of a frog engaged in some athletic pursuit. He mentioned your name at that time and indicated that he valued highly the lengthy correspondence with you over the past several years.

I will do what I can to suggest his sponsorship of your bills.

Sincerely,

Paul N. McCloskey, Jr.

PNMcC:cb
cc: Honorable Jerome Waldie

JEROME R. WALDIE
MEMBER OF CONGRESS
14TH DISTRICT, CALIFORNIA

WASHINGTON ADDRESS:
ROOM 408
CANNON HOUSE OFFICE BUILDING
WASHINGTON, D.C. 20515
PHONE: 225-5911
AREA CODE: 202

COMMITTEES:
JUDICIARY
POST OFFICE AND CIVIL SERVICE
SELECT COMMITTEE ON CRIME

DISTRICT REPRESENTATIVE:
E. A. "PAT" FERGUSON
P.O. Box 864
CIVIC CENTER
CONCORD, CALIFORNIA 94520
PHONE: 687-1200
AREA CODE: 415

RICHMOND OFFICE:
3915 MACDONALD AVENUE
RICHMOND, CALIFORNIA 94805
PHONE: 233-4425

Congress of the United States
House of Representatives
Washington, D.C. 20515

June 3, 1971

Mr. Nestle J. Frobish
Lyndonville, Vermont 05851

Dear Mr. Frobish:

Apparently, our Omnibus Frog Bill is producing some moments of anxiety within the citadels of the Department of Interior. I have yet to receive a response from my request for their analysis of this complex measure. I'll await their reply only a bit longer and then will ask that great Chairman of the Interior Committee, Wayne Aspinall, to review and comment.

In the meantime, I wish to report on your vigorous campaign to procure co-authors for this Bill. Pete McCloskey has indicated cautious sympathy for the objectives of the bill, but, in all honesty, I take credit for even that tepid expression of approval. I sought his assistance on the way back from Indochina when he was in a physically and emotionally weakened condition. But, other than that, you haven't produced much support.

I also enclose several clippings indicating a rather global interest in the subject matter of this measure. One is from a Hong Kong paper and the other a UPI release from Moscow.

I do think the youngsters in England deserve particular commendation.

Sincerely yours,

Jerry Waldie

JEROME R. WALDIE

JRW:afs
enc.

WORLDWIDE FAIRPLAY FOR FROGS COMMITTEE

MA N OFF CE
LYNDONV LE VERMONT
*   *
OVERSEAS OFFICE
REDCOATS GREEN, ENGLAND

DISTRICT OFFICES
BERKELEY, CALIF.
MARTINEZ, CALIF.
SANTA CRUZ,CALIF.
NEW HAVEN, CONN.
CAMBRIDGE, MASS.
AUSTIN, TEXAS
WASHINGTON, D.C.

Lyndonville, Vt. 05851

June 6, 1971

Hon. Jerome Waldie
House Office Building
Washington, D.C. 20515

Dear Congressman Waldie:

I certainly cannot understand why the Interior Department is being so dilatory in analyzing your Omnibus Frog Protection Act. After all, President Nixon has said he intends to preserve the environment, and to my way of

FAIR PLAY FOR FROGS

thinking, an environment without frogs is not an environment that has been preserved. Since the Secretary of the Interior works for President Nixon—at least this one works for him—why hasn't the department come out foursquare in favor of the bill?

On the congressional front, I think we are doing wonderfully. The leading sponsor is a man who has been a candidate for the highest post in the House, and our new-found supporter is a man who is running for the other party's presidential nomination! This combination is certainly going to make lots of people take notice! However, I should point out that beyond writing extraordinarily persuasive letters, floor speeches included, for illustrious members of Congress, I am not in a position to undertake the vigorous day-to-day lobbying effort needed to line up supporters. That is your job, Mr. Congressman! I will of course be happy to write letters to any member you may name, telling him of your sterling leadership in this field and urging his support of your bill.

The clippings on frog-lovers' activities from around the world are of course appreciated, although my clipping service gets most of them. I have written a few remarks on the English article which you rightly find so commendable, for I am sure you will want to put this in the *Record*. Please send me a copy as soon as it appears.

Yours truly,

Nestle J Frobish

Nestle J. Frobish

JEROME R. WALDIE
MEMBER OF CONGRESS
14TH DISTRICT, CALIFORNIA

WASHINGTON ADDRESS:
Room 408
Cannon House Office Building
Washington, D.C. 20515
Phone: 225-8911
Area Code: 202

COMMITTEES:
JUDICIARY
POST OFFICE AND CIVIL SERVICE
SELECT COMMITTEE ON CRIME

DISTRICT REPRESENTATIVE:
E. A. "Pat" Ferguson
P.O. Box 864
Civic Center
Concord, California 94520
Phone: 687-1200
Area Code: 415

Richmond Office:
3915 Macdonald Avenue
Richmond, California 94806
Phone: 233-4425

Congress of the United States
House of Representatives
Washington, D.C. 20515

June 10, 1971

Mr. Nestle J. Frobish
Lyndonville, Vermont 05851

Dear Mr. Frobish:

Your suggested entry into the *Congressional Record* of an article commending some English children for their compassionate acts involving the sex life of toads is acknowledged.

I think I will not put it into the *Record*.

Sincerely yours,

Jerry Waldie

JEROME R. WALDIE
United States Congressman
Fourteenth District

JRW/ml

WORLDWIDE FAIRPLAY FOR FROGS COMMITTEE

MAIN OFFICE
LYNDONVILLE, VERMONT
*   *
OVERSEAS OFFICE
REDCOATS GREEN, ENGLAND

DISTRICT OFFICES
BERKELEY, CALIF.
MARTINEZ, CALIF.
SANTA CRUZ, CALIF.
NEW HAVEN, CONN.
CAMBRIDGE, MASS.
AUSTIN, TEXAS
WASHINGTON, D.C.

Lyndonville, Vt. 05851

June 16, 1971

Hon. Jerome Waldie
House Office Building
Washington, D. C.

Dear Congressman Waldie:

I am shocked by your abrupt refusal to call to the attention of your colleagues the fine work of the Redcoats Heath toad patrol, and the rather acerbic tone of your letter of June 10. After all, in your letter of June 3 you wrote, God strike me dead if you didn't, "I do think the youngsters in England deserve particular commendation."

Now how, I ask you, are they to receive this commendation when the only people in the U. S. A. who know about their meritorious deeds are you, an illustrious member of Congress, and me, an unhappily obscure battler for frogdom—obscure, that is, to the unthinking general public who has not yet got into the frog thing? That was your idea, to commend these young folks, and I think if you have any pretension to perseverance and principle, you should carry through and make sure they get the particular commendation you have unequivocally stated that they deserve.

Please send me immediately a list of your colleagues

who I can write to persuade to join in your crusade. You will still have to persuade them in person in the cloakrooms, of course, but I can soften them up in advance. I will probably start with Honorable Wayne Aspinall, who you so obviously admire and respect. I am sure when he hears this bill means more to you than anything, he will bring his committee around quickly.

Yours truly,

Nestle J. Frobish

Nestle J. Frobish

JEROME R. WALDIE
MEMBER OF CONGRESS
14TH DISTRICT, CALIFORNIA

WASHINGTON ADDRESS:
ROOM 406
CANNON HOUSE OFFICE BUILDING
WASHINGTON, D.C. 20515
PHONE: 225-5511
AREA CODE: 202

COMMITTEES:
JUDICIARY
POST OFFICE AND CIVIL SERVICE
SELECT COMMITTEE ON CRIME

DISTRICT REPRESENTATIVE:
E. A. "PAT" FERGUSON
P.O. BOX 864
CIVIC CENTER
CONCORD, CALIFORNIA 94520
PHONE: 687-1200
AREA CODE: 415

RICHMOND OFFICE:
3915 MACDONALD AVENUE
RICHMOND, CALIFORNIA 94805
PHONE: 233-4425

Congress of the United States
House of Representatives
Washington, D.C. 20515

June 18, 1971

Mr. Nestle J. Frobish
Lyndonville, Vermont 05851

Dear Mr. Frobish:

I have received your letter of June 16th and I had thought that my suggestion that "the youngsters in England deserve particular commendation" would be understood as a suggestion that you extend that commendation. I can hardly believe they would equate a Congressional commendation with words of praise from you. You apparently are less sensitive to suggestion than I had anticipated. Henceforth, I will be more direct in my correspondence.

In that regard, I can only suggest one other Congressman who might be inclined to fulfill a responsibility that should be yours, Mr. Bill Hathaway from Maine.

I do not believe Chairman Aspinall feels about frogs the way you do. His "bag" tends to deal with frog habitations, such as sloughs, rivers and swamps, and his concern with those habitations tends more toward drying them up or damming them than improving their frog beneficial characteristics.

Sincerely yours,

JEROME R. WALDIE
United States Congressman
Fourteenth District

JRW/ml

WORLDWIDE FAIRPLAY FOR FROGS
COMMITTEE

MAIN OFFICE
LYNDONVILLE, VERMONT
*   *
OVERSEAS OFFICE
REDCOATS GREEN, ENGLAND

DISTRICT OFFICES
BERKELEY, CALIF.
MARTINEZ, CALIF.
SANTA CRUZ, CALIF.
NEW HAVEN, CONN.
CAMBRIDGE, MASS.
AUSTIN, TEXAS
WASHINGTON, D.C.

Lyndonville, Vt. 05851

June 27, 1971

Hon. William Hathaway
House Office Building
Washington, D. C. 20515

Dear Congressman Hathaway:

Congressman Jerome Waldie badly needs your help but apparently is too bashful to ask for it.

You may be unaware of this fact, but ten years ago Congressman Waldie, then a rising young assemblyman from Antioch, California, introduced a bill in the California Assembly to create new ways for murdering frogs. "Frogs," it read, "may be taken by using a slingshot." What prompted Mr. Waldie to become the champion of the frog murderers of his assembly district is not known to me, but he now, after ten years of relentless reform efforts by me, claims to be a friend of frogs and has asked to be shriven, again by me, for his past transgressions.

I accordingly drafted up the "Omnibus Frog Protection Act of 1971" for his introduction, to once and for all purge himself of accumulated sin. I even drafted floor speeches for various worthy members, like Mr. Albert,

FAIR PLAY FOR FROGS

Mr. Boggs, Mr. Ford, and Mr. H. R. Gross, endorsing this vital piece of legislation and commending Mr. Waldie for his leadership. Mr. Waldie, however, has a problem. He is faint of heart. He fails to realize the fact that a host of frog-lovers the nation over will utter a mighty croak of support the minute he acts. Perhaps Mr. Waldie still recalls the monumental silence that greeted his candidacy for Speaker a while back. You, Congressman, can convince him of the timeliness of this act, and of the full throated support he will immediately receive. Rep. Paul McCloskey, a Republican who among other things is now running for President, has endorsed this grand effort to protect the humble frog. I look to you, Congressman, to roar down from the frog-bejeweled Allagash and inspire Mr. Waldie to great deeds, for which his character presently seems to lack the resolution.

Yours truly,

Nestle J Frobish

Nestle J. Frobish
Chairman

FAIR PLAY FOR FROGS

WiLLIAM D. HATHAWAY
2D District, MAINE

COMMITTEE
ON
APPROPRIATIONS

Congress of the United States
House of Representatives
Washington, D.C. 20515

June 30, 1971

Honorable Jerome Waldie
House of Representatives
Washington, D. C.

Dear Jerry:
Is this for real?

Sincerely,

William D. Hathaway
U. S. Congressman

WDH/em
Encl.

How could you be so frogetful?

JEROME R. WALDIE
MEMBER OF CONGRESS
14TH DISTRICT, CALIFORNIA

WASHINGTON ADDRESS:
Room 408
CANNON HOUSE OFFICE BUILDING
WASHINGTON, D.C. 20515
PHONE: 225-5811
AREA CODE: 202

COMMITTEES:
JUDICIARY
POST OFFICE AND CIVIL SERVICE
SELECT COMMITTEE ON CRIME

DISTRICT REPRESENTATIVE:
E. A. "PAT" FERGUSON
P.O. Box 864
CIVIC CENTER
CONCORD, CALIFORNIA 94520
PHONE: 687-1200
AREA CODE: 415

RICHMOND OFFICE:
3915 MACDONALD AVENUE
RICHMOND, CALIFORNIA 94805
PHONE: 233-4425

Congress of the United States
House of Representatives
Washington, D.C. 20515

July 8, 1971

Mr. Nestle J. Frobish, Chairman
Worldwide Fair Play for Frogs Committee
Lyndonville, Vermont 05851

Dear Mr. Frobish:

I enclose a note that I received from Congressman Hathaway enclosing a copy of your letter to him wherein you had less than complimentary remarks concerning my efforts on behalf of frogs.

Not only am I apparently to be plagued by your correspondence, but now, as you will see from the note on Mr. Hathaway's letter, I apparently am to be plagued by a punster.

It is difficult for me to determine which correspondence offends me the most.

Sincerely yours,

JEROME R. WALDIE

JRW:afs
CC: Congressman William D. Hathaway

July 31, 1971
CONGRESSIONAL RECORD—Extensions of Remarks E8663

Frobish Honored

HON. JEROME R. WALDIE
of California
in the House of Representatives
Friday, July 30, 1971
MR. WALDIE. Mr. Speaker, Voltaire once proclaimed:
Arguing with a fool proves there are two.

No one I know has had the sense nor the stamina to disagree with Nestle J. Frobish, a former constituent of mine who today receives a rare honor.

Mr. Frobish, known for his deep croaky voice and sudden leaping style of motion has been recognized by his peers as a symbol of high standards in literary creativity and the dramatic arts. The Students for a Better Society, a group of committed young writers from the University of California at Santa Cruz, has adopted a resolution urging the appropriate authorities to name the fifth college of their campus after Mr. Frobish. No longer will Mr. Frobish be the biggest frog in a small pond. The resolution follows:

Resolution

Whereas: College V has operated for two years without an official name

Whereas: The college's main emphasis includes the literary and dramatic arts

Whereas: Nestle J. Frobish has consistently been associated with great works of fiction

Be it Resolved: That College V of the University of

FAIR PLAY FOR FROGS

California at Santa Cruz take the name, Nestle J. Frobish,
to honor Lyndonville, Vermont's most favorite son.
Attest:

> John Laird,
> > President.
> Charles Koppelman,
> > Vice-President I.
> Bob Bilex,
> > Vice-President II.
> Dave Tenzir,
> > Vice-President III.
> Sue Grabowski,
> > Ex-Officio member.

---

17 July 1971

> Frog Defense League of Yorkshire
> Ingle Wood
> Hyde Park Road
> Harrogate, Yorkshire, U. K.

Mr. Jerome Waldie M. C.
U. S. Capitol
Washington, D. C., U. S. A.

Dear Mr. Waldie:

Your interest in and commendation of those outstanding young people of Redcoats Heath who are selflessly
convoying toads across the busy highway was made
known here and in the view of us defenders of frogs, you
suddenly vaulted from obscurity to an ascending importance among the emerging pro-frog statesmen of the
world.

Imagine then our shock and dismay when we learned

that despite your private sentiments, assuming they were genuine, you were unwilling to call this example of inspiring service to the attention of the Americans who eagerly seek out your remarks in the congressional publication.

Those bright-eyed little children, Master Charles Glue and his sister Christine, who had provided the leadership for this project, were at first elated at your interest, then utterly crushed by your callous hypocrisy. Christine in fact cried for three days and finally had to be given sedatives. Charles has appeared listless and there is some concern for his health.

As a result of this turn of events, the Frog Defense League of Yorkshire has given its recent collection of £2 3s. 6d. to the Glue family for medical and psychiatric expenses. This is the money we initially collected to send to you to help finance your next race for Speaker of the House.

If our present judgment of you is in error, please advise us accordingly, enclosing a copy of your remarks from the *Congressional Record* paying tribute to the Glues.
Yours,

Frederick L. Meacham
General Secretary

WORLDWIDE FAIRPLAY FOR FROGS COMMITTEE

MAIN OFFICE
LYNDONVILLE, VERMONT
•   •
OVERSEAS OFFICE:
REDCOATS GREEN, ENGLAND

DISTRICT OFFICES
BERKELEY, CALIF.
MARTINEZ, CALIF.
SANTA CRUZ, CALIF.
NEW HAVEN, CONN.
CAMBRIDGE, MASS.
AUSTIN, TEXAS
WASHINGTON, D.C.

Lyndonville, Vt. 05851
August 8, 1971

Governor Ronald Reagan
Board of Regents, State College System
Sacramento, California

Dear Governor Reagan:

The Students for a Better Society at the University of Santa Cruz recently adopted a resolution asking you to name College V on that campus after me, Nestle J. Frobish, Friend of Frogs. Your friend and admirer Congressman Jerome Waldie is squarely behind this proposal and has put it in the *Congressional Record.* I just wanted you to know that if the Board of Regents decides to do this, I accept.

From a political standpoint, Governor, it might not be a bad idea if you followed the students' suggestion. In the first place, it does not take much to get California students to riot these days, so why give them one more grievance and fan the flames?

Besides, there is some reason to believe that Congressman Waldie wants to focus this issue, so that if you fail to respond he will use it to oust you from the governor's mansion, if any. You wouldn't want to have to face thousands of enraged frog-lovers, spurred on by Mr. Waldie, in an election year, would you?

FAIR PLAY FOR FROGS

So if you go ahead and do this, I think everyone will be happy—you, the students, and me. Of course, Mr. Waldie may not be happy that you took away his issue, but that's his problem, right?

Yours truly,

Nestle J. Frobish

Nestle J. Frobish

WORLDWIDE FAIRPLAY FOR FROGS COMMITTEE

MAIN OFFICE
LYNDONVILLE, VERMONT
* *
OVERSEAS OFFICE
REDCOATS GREEN, ENGLAND

DISTRICT OFFICES
BERKELEY, CALIF.
MARTINEZ, CALIF.
SANTA CRUZ, CALIF.
NEW HAVEN, CONN.
CAMBRIDGE, MASS.
AUSTIN, TEXAS
WASHINGTON, D.C.

Lyndonville, Vt. 05851
August 9, 1971

Hon. Jerome Waldie
House Office Bldg.
Washington, D. C. 20515

Dear Mr. Waldie:

You have certainly developed the knack of talking out of miscellaneous sides of your mouth to appease different viewpoints—so much so, in fact, that you should probably run for governor of California. In fact, I hear you are. I refer of course to your letter to Mr. Rubin of San Diego, California, who will presumably vote in the next gubernatorial contest there. For your information, Mr. Rubin, sometimes known as "The Great Rubini," is an accomplished frog murderer—just the nefarious sort of person who contributed to your anti-frog fixation ten years ago.

FAIR PLAY FOR FROGS

Your continued attempts to appease such persons will only destroy your precarious credibility with the lovers of frogs.

There is some hope on the legislative front, however. The state of New Hampshire recently banned the use of crossbows for taking fish. They are getting close to the real issue. I understand that the House Interior Committee is presently completing work on a bill to further protect wild burros and mustangs. When this bill reaches the floor, you will have a marvelous chance to offer the Omnibus Frog Protection Act as an amendment. Hundreds of thousands of frog-lovers the nation over, lots of whom will be voting in California gubernatorials, will have their eyes on you to Act Boldly.

I have duly noted your entry in the *Record* of the resolution by the Students for a Better Society to name the fifth college at Santa Cruz after me, Nestle J. Frobish, friend of frogs. While I could hardly deny my association with literary creativity and the dramatic arts, and while I could hardly refuse the honor proffered, I wish to point out that The Cause is All Important, and those of us who have struggled in it are but grains of chaff in the cosmic wind. Let's get that bill passed, and it will be a fitting monument to your illustrious congressional career. Incidentally, have you ever gotten a bill passed?

Congressman Hathaway is such a foul speller that he may not be much help in our cause. But in any case, you should straighten him out at the first opportunity. Who else would you like me to exhort?

Yours for Bold Action Now for Frogdom, and Depending Upon your Success in That, the Governorship, Later,

Nestle

Nestle

JEROME R. WALDIE
MEMBER OF CONGRESS
14TH DISTRICT, CALIFORNIA

WASHINGTON ADDRESS:
ROOM 408
CANNON HOUSE OFFICE BUILDING
WASHINGTON, D.C. 20515
PHONE: 225-5511
AREA CODE: 202

COMMITTEES:
JUDICIARY
POST OFFICE AND CIVIL SERVICE
SELECT COMMITTEE ON CRIME

DISTRICT REPRESENTATIVE:
E. A. "PAT" FERGUSON
P.O. BOX 864
CIVIC CENTER
CONCORD, CALIFORNIA 94520
PHONE: 687-1200
AREA CODE: 415

RICHMOND OFFICE:
3915 MACDONALD AVENUE
RICHMOND, CALIFORNIA 94805
PHONE: 233-4425

Congress of the United States
House of Representatives
Washington, D.C. 20515

August 20, 1971

Mr. Nestle J. Frobish
Worldwide Fair Play for Frogs Committee
Lyndonville, Vermont 05851

Dear Mr. Frobish:

I have your letter of August 9th before me.

I do not recall meeting you personally nor do I consider our correspondence to have resulted in any personal relationship.

Yet you presume and sign your letter to me "Nestle."

Please maintain in future correspondence a less intimate stance that will reflect what I insist to be the accurate state of our relationship.

Sincerely yours,

Jerry Waldie

JEROME R. WALDIE
United States Congressman
Fourteenth District

JRW/ml

FAIR PLAY FOR FROGS

UNIVERSITY OF CALIFORNIA, SANTA CRUZ

BERKELEY · DAVIS · IRVINE · LOS ANGELES · RIVERSIDE · SAN DIEGO · SAN FRANCISCO   SANTA BARBARA · SANTA CRUZ

UNIVERSITY RELATIONS   SANTA CRUZ, CALIFORNIA   95060

August 19, 1971

The Honorable Jerome R. Waldie
House Office Building
Washington, D. C. 20515

Dear Congressman Waldie:

Mrs. Lewis in your Martinez office suggested I get in touch with you regarding correspondence you entered in the July 31, 1971 *Congressional Record*. It had to do with the naming of College Five here on the campus of the University of California, Santa Cruz.

Ever since hearing about the idea of naming College Five after someone called Nestle J. Frobish (a long-time acquaintance of yours, according to Charles Koppelman), I have been curious as to his identity and source of prominence.

All investigation so far seems to indicate that Frobish is a frog!

As for the naming of College Five at UC, Santa Cruz I assure you that everyone on this campus would very much like to see the name changed to something more personal.

As you may know, the different cluster colleges at Santa Cruz are constructed with State and other public funds, but that certain "augmenting" facilities, such as a home for the head of the college and his family, quarters for some of the faculty, special student lounges, a library–reading room, and so forth are paid for by private money.

Since College Five is still in search of a donor of the

required $1,000,000 the name of the place is left open for the discretion of its eventual benefactor.

The other five college communities on the campus have personal names: Cowell, Stevenson, Crown, Merrill, and Kresge—mostly all named after family foundations. The enclosed map guide has a bit more information on how the colleges are funded.

Anything you can tell me about Frobish will be greatly appreciated. Perhaps he or his friends may turn out to have the makings of a donor after all.

Sincerely,

Tom O'Leary

Encl.

WORLDWIDE FAIRPLAY FOR FROGS COMMITTEE

MAIN OFFICE
LYNDONVILLE, VERMONT
* *
OVERSEAS OFFICE:
REDCOATS GREEN, ENGLAND

DISTRICT OFFICES:
BERKELEY, CALIF.
MARTINEZ, CALIF.
SANTA CRUZ, CALIF.
NEW HAVEN, CONN.
CAMBRIDGE, MASS.
AUSTIN, TEXAS
WASHINGTON, D.C.

Lyndonville, Vt. 05851

August 30, 1971

Hon. Jerome R. Waldie
House Office Building
Washington, D. C.

Dear Jerome:

Some truculent lout on your staff sent me a ridiculous letter objecting to my signing a letter to you as "Nestle." The reason I know it was some flunkey, and not you, was

FAIR PLAY FOR FROGS

that your letter was signed "Jerome R. Waldie," not "Jerry Waldie," the signature used on your letters to me of May 14 and June 14, 1969, March 30, July 14 and September 11, 1970, and January 4, April 6, June 3, June 10, June 13, July 8, and July 15, 1971. I trust this person will be dismissed promptly.

Actually, my really close friends, other than frogs, of course, call me "Ned," which I am told is an acronym for three Serbo-Croatian words meaning "Righter of Wrongs, Purveyor of Wisdom, Friend of Frogs." When you are fully shriven, you may feel free to do the same.

Your campaign to save the frogs, attenuated and half-hearted as it appears to be, seems to be getting some people interested. One of my operatives uncovered the enclosed note recently. Keep at it. We will win.

Yours truly,

Nestle J. Frobish

THE WHITE HOUSE

WASHINGTON

17 Aug. 71

TO: Whitaker
FROM: HALDEMAN
The Old Man says to be sure that this fellow Waldie doesn't steal the frog issue from us.

JEROME R. WALDIE
MEMBER OF CONGRESS
14TH DISTRICT, CALIFORNIA

WASHINGTON ADDRESS:
Room 408
Cannon House Office Building
Washington, D.C. 20515
Phone: 225-5511
Area Code: 202

COMMITTEES:
JUDICIARY
POST OFFICE AND CIVIL SERVICE
SELECT COMMITTEE ON CRIME

DISTRICT REPRESENTATIVE:
E. A. "Pat" Ferguson
P.O. Box 864
Civic Center
Concord, California 94520
Phone: 687-1200
Area Code: 415

Richmond Office:
3915 Macdonald Avenue
Richmond, California 94805
Phone: 233-4425

Congress of the United States

House of Representatives

Washington, D.C. 20515

September 2, 1971

Mr. Tom O'Leary
c/o University Relations
University of California
Santa Cruz, California

Dear Mr. O'Leary:

I must say I am somewhat disappointed that the policy of naming campuses in our State University is so heavily

FAIR PLAY FOR FROGS

dependent upon donations from the recipient of that honor.

Nonetheless, recognizing the incredible financial difficulties into which our educational system has been plunged in the last few years, I can accept the condition of $1,000,000 to have Campus 5 named the "Nestle J. Frobish College."

I will seek assistance among those who are interested in pursuing this matter to determine the best manner by which we might accumulate the $1,000,000.

A number of suggestions are presently under consideration, not the least of which is a Frogs'-leg Fry to be held on Bethel Island in the Sacramento–San Joaquin River Delta area in my Congressional District. It is perhaps overly optimistic to believe that we can sell a million tickets at $1.00 each, but as I understand it that will be the effort that will be extended.

May I consider you as a prospect for the purchase of a portion of those tickets?

I cannot tell you a great deal about Nestle J. Frobish as you have requested, except that his concern for creatures on this earth who are less privileged than most of us is commendable and touching. Further, his skill in advocating their consideration is unsurpassed, and I am thoroughly convinced that even without raising $1,000,-000 the honor of having Campus 5 named after him would be richly deserved.

I will be in touch with you further as the plans to raise the necessary monies to buy this privilege progress.

Sincerely yours,

Jerry Waldie

JEROME R. WALDIE, M. C.

JRW:afs
CC: Mr. Nestle J. Frobish

WORLDWIDE FAIRPLAY FOR FROGS COMMITTEE

MAIN OFFICE
LYNDONVILLE, VERMONT
* *
OVERSEAS OFFICE
REDCOATS GREEN, ENGLAND

DISTRICT OFFICES
BERKELEY, CALIF.
MARTINEZ, CALIF.
SANTA CRUZ, CALIF.
NEW HAVEN, CONN.
CAMBRIDGE, MASS.
AUSTIN, TEXAS
WASHINGTON, D.C.

Lyndonville, Vt. 05851

September 14, 1971

Honorable Jerome Waldie
House Office Building
Washington, D. C.

Dear Congressman:

I am certain that it will be a relatively minor matter to raise the $1,000,000 required to bribe the California State College system to name College Five at Santa Cruz after that unparalleled friend of frogs, me, Nestle J. Frobish. All we need to do is galvanize the latent pro-frog sentiments among the American people, plus whatever can be scraped up over at Redcoats Heath, England, from the local frog patrol. This task will be accomplished handily by your introduction of the Omnibus Frog Protection Act and making it a national issue, which I am sure is well within your power even before you rise to the governorship of your state. I think this would be a lot safer and surer—raising as little as 25¢ each from 4 million friends of frogs, rather than getting $1 from 1 million people out to Bethel Island for a gala feed. Go to it, and Godspeed!

This was probably inadvertent on your part, but I think I should point out that having fried frogs' legs as the main course at that Bethel Island event is not exactly in keeping with the spirit of the campaign, now, is it? I mean people seem to be confused enough in this age of complex national issues without your proposing a frogs'-leg dinner for 1 million friends of frogs.

Incidentally, I am told that the so-called unnamed college Five at Santa Cruz is actually named after Thurgood P. Five, a notorious 19th-century gig manufacturer of Poontang, California. I know you will want to erase this vile commemoration with great celerity.

Yours truly,

Nestle J. Frobish

Nestle J. Frobish

WORLDWIDE FAIRPLAY FOR FROGS
COMMITTEE

MAIN OFFICE
LYNDONVILLE, VERMONT
* *
OVERSEAS OFFICE
REDCOATS GREEN, ENGLAND

DISTRICT OFFICES
BERKELEY, CALIF.
MARTINEZ, CALIF.
SANTA CRUZ, CALIF.
NEW HAVEN, CONN.
CAMBRIDGE, MASS.
AUSTIN, TEXAS
WASHINGTON, D.C.

Lyndonville, Vt. 05851
November 2, 1971

Hon. Jerome Waldie
House Office Building
Washington, D. C.

Dear Congressman Waldie:

Inasmuch as I have not heard any startling good news from you in the last few weeks with respect to the save-the-frog campaign you are leading, I can only assume

FAIR PLAY FOR FROGS

that you are in need, once again, of additional inspiration.

Note the attached page from the *Congressional Record*, which contains an entry entitled "Can the Whale Be Saved?" by Senator Church of Idaho.

Now Senator Church is no dummy. I cannot suppose there are an inordinate number of whale-lovers in Idaho, but Senator Church is making damn sure they will vote for *him*, Friend of Whales.

Now I ask you, Congressman, how many frog-lovers are there in the state of California? Even netted against a small and iniquitous band of frog-haters, with whom, I recall, you used to traffic, at least in election years, the actual number virtually defies calculation!

Wouldn't you like to have this vast aggregation—or even half of it—join the enthusiastic, and equally half-vast, aggregation that has swept you to electoral victory in your previous sorties? Of course you would. Especially since you apparently have ambition to rise to one-knows-not-what positions of power and eminence.

So, let's get the old Omnibus Frog Protection Act in the old hopper, P.D.Q. Aside from the wonders it will do for frogdom, it may well catapult you into national prominence overnight. In fact, I am reasonably sure it will. And you will also have the warm feeling that comes from knowing that, while you are on duty in Washington every frog in America, and their lovers, sleeps a little more soundly every night.

Packing paper Packing paper,*

Nestle J. Frobish

Nestle J. Frobish
* This is the anglicized version of a Greek word meaning "onward and upward," I am told. Excelsior?

PAUL N. McCLOSKEY, JR.
11TH DISTRICT, CALIFORNIA

COMMITTEE ON
GOVERNMENT OPERATIONS
AND
COMMITTEE ON
MERCHANT MARINE
AND FISHERIES

Congress of the United States
House of Representatives
Washington, D.C. 20515

November 8, 1971

Mr. John Laird
Santa Cruz, California 05960

Dear John:

I much appreciated your letter of August 20 regarding Nestle J. Frobish. I know and respect Mr. Frobish highly, but am dubious about naming the college of the University of California at Santa Cruz after him. Mr. Frobish is a man of deep sensibilities and great concern for the betterment of mankind, animal life and the world's environment. His modesty would probably cause him to withdraw completely from the public stage on which he performs so well, were he required to accept the plaudits and hosannas of a grateful citizenry upon the dedication of the new college.

If you could ever have the privilege of seeing Mr. Frobish at the edge of his secluded personal frog pond in northern Vermont, you would understand my concern that his distinguished contributions to the world remain unpublicized.

Respectfully,

Paul N. McCloskey, Jr.

PNMcC:nn

JEROME R. WALDIE
MEMBER OF CONGRESS
14th District, California

WASHINGTON ADDRESS:
Room 406
Cannon House Office Building
Washington, D.C. 20515
Phone: 225-5511
Area Code: 202

COMMITTEES:
JUDICIARY
POST OFFICE AND CIVIL SERVICE
SELECT COMMITTEE ON CRIME

DISTRICT REPRESENTATIVE,
E. A. "Pat" Ferguson
P.O. Box 864
Civic Center
Concord, California 94520
Phone: 687-1200
Area Code: 415

Richmond Office:
3915 MacDonald Avenue
Richmond, California 94805
Phone: 233-4485

Congress of the United States
House of Representatives
Washington, D.C. 20515

November 18, 1971

Mr. Nestle J. Frobish
Lyndonville, Vt. 05851

Dear Mr. Frobish:

That I am in need of additional inspiration with regard to the save-the-frog campaign is accurately recorded in the remark contained in your letter. That your letter itself is sufficient to provide such inspiration would be an unwarranted presumption on your part.

Sincerely,

JEROME R. WALDIE

JRW:mg

WORLDWIDE FAIRPLAY FOR FROGS COMMITTEE

MAIN OFFICE
LYNDONVILLE, VERMONT
• •
OVERSEAS OFFICE
REDCOATS GREEN, ENGLAND

DISTRICT OFFICES
BERKELEY, CALIF.
MARTINEZ, CALIF.
SANTA CRUZ, CALIF.
NEW HAVEN, CONN.
CAMBRIDGE, MASS.
AUSTIN, TEXAS
WASHINGTON, D.C.

Lyndonville, Vt. 05851

November 27, 1971

Mr. Allen Cherry
Success Motivation Institute
Waco, Texas

Dear Mr. Cherry:

I am writing on behalf of Congressman Jerome R. Waldie of California, who badly needs the kind of motivation that I understand your organization can provide.

Mr. Waldie used to be quite hostile to frogs. After a decade of relentless persuasion by me, he became sort of a friend of frogs, but apparently lack of motivation has held him back from making a real name for himself in this important field.

I would appreciate it, as would all frog-lovers everywhere, if you would contact Mr. Waldie and offer to design a program for him to better motivate his currently feeble efforts on behalf of the humble frog.

Please let me know how it works out.

Yours truly,

Nestle J. Frobish

Nestle J. Frobish

Leadership Motivation Institute PAUL J. MEYER, PRESIDENT
a Division of Success Motivation®Institute, Inc., "Motivating People to Their Full Potential"®

December 6, 1971

Representative Jerome R. Waldie
House of Representatives
Washington, D. C.

Dear Congressman Waldie,

I have just received a letter from a Mr. Nestle Frobish, of Lyndonville, Vermont, stating that you were once quite hostile to frogs, then abandoned your hostility, and are now on the verge of being a great friend of frogs. According to Mr. Frobish, all you need is the proper motivation. Mr. Frobish also says that he seems unable to inspire you sufficiently in this direction, and has asked us to contact you about enrolling in our Leadership Motivation program.

While most of our customers have used our course to gain greater rewards in their business and professional lives, I see no reason why the same techniques could not be applied to make you a real leader on behalf of what Mr. Frobish refers to as "the humble frog." This is unusual enough to provoke our interest, and I would be pleased to make a special effort to meet with you on my next trip

FAIR PLAY FOR FROGS

to Washington to explain how Success Motivation can make you into not only a friend of frogs, but a real Champion of Frogs!

If this is your goal, please let me know.

Yours truly,

Allen Cherry

Allen Cherry

cc: Mr. Nestle J. Frobish

JEROME R. WALDIE
MEMBER OF CONGRESS
14TH DISTRICT, CALIFORNIA

WASHINGTON ADDRESS:
ROOM 408
CANNON HOUSE OFFICE BUILDING
WASHINGTON, D.C. 20515
PHONE: 225-5811
AREA CODE: 202

COMMITTEES:
JUDICIARY
POST OFFICE AND CIVIL SERVICE
SELECT COMMITTEE ON CRIME

DISTRICT REPRESENTATIVE:
E. A. "PAT" FERGUSON
P.O. BOX 864
CIVIC CENTER
CONCORD, CALIFORNIA 94520
PHONE: 687-1200
AREA CODE: 415

RICHMOND OFFICE:
3915 MACDONALD AVENUE
RICHMOND, CALIFORNIA 94805
PHONE: 233-4428

Congress of the United States
House of Representatives
Washington, D.C. 20515

December 14, 1971

Mr. Allen Cherry
Leadership Motivation Institute
Waco, Texas 76710

Dear Mr. Cherry:

Whatever my goals may be I would not seek assistance in furthering them from a signator on company stationery whose status is such that his name is not found on the letterhead.

Sincerely yours,

JEROME R. WALDIE
United States Congressman
Fourteenth District

JRW/vjw

WORLDWIDE FAIRPLAY FOR FROGS COMMITTEE

MAIN OFFICE
LYNDONVILLE, VERMONT
*   *
OVERSEAS OFFICE
REDCOATS GREEN, ENGLAND

DISTRICT OFFICES
BERKELEY, CALIF.
MARTINEZ, CALIF.
SANTA CRUZ, CALIF.
NEW HAVEN, CONN.
CAMBRIDGE, MASS.
AUSTIN, TEXAS
WASHINGTON, D.C.

Lyndonville, Vermont 05851

January 31, 1972

Hon. Jerome Waldie
House Office Building
Washington, D. C.

Dear Congressman Waldie:

I read your remarks in the *Record* on the Contra Costa sand pits (January 18) and can wholeheartedly say that you are doing a truly outstanding job. America needs more men like you in high office. You are a great inspiration to our youth, and a worthy successor to George Washington.

FAIR PLAY FOR FROGS

Aw, what's the use, Waldie, let's face it: you aren't getting anything done. The initial euphoria of your initial—and provisional—shriving has long since worn off. No progress is being made. The humble frog stands in greater danger every day, while you stand idly by at best, and perpetrating horrors the world not yet knows what, at worst.

In addition to failing to take a leadership role with the Omnibus Frog Protection Act, which I so generously provided you as a part of your long-sought-for shriving, you also missed the boat on Public Law 92-159. This was the law which provided a criminal penalty for shooting certain fauna from aircraft. True, it could be interpreted to cover frogs but a Waldie amendment to mention frogs explicitly would no doubt have removed later obstacles to convictions of aerial frog-hunters, stemming from legal uncertainties and incomplete legislative history.

The time is come when you must make a fundamental decision, vital to your future career: are you going to work for the friends of the Contra Costa sand pits, or the friends of frogs? Or are you going to work at all? Hundreds of thousands of frog-lovers stand quivering in expectation of your strong affirmation of ranaphilia, for which, you are fond of reminding one and all, you once received an award.

All a-quiver,

Nestle J Frobish

Nestle J. Frobish

WORLDWIDE FAIRPLAY FOR FROGS COMMITTEE

MAIN OFFICE
LYNDONVILLE, VERMONT
• •
OVERSEAS OFFICE:
REDCOATS GREEN, ENGLAND

DISTRICT OFFICES
BERKELEY, CALIF.
MARTINEZ, CALIF.
SANTA CRUZ, CALIF.
NEW HAVEN, CONN.
CAMBRIDGE, MASS.
AUSTIN, TEXAS
WASHINGTON, D.C.

Lyndonville, Vt. 05851
February 5, 1972

Arthur Hoppe, Ace Newsman
San Francisco Chronicle
San Francisco, California 94119

Dear Art:

Our mutual acquaintance, Jerome Waldie, putative friend of frogs, is badly in need of motivation.

He is still sitting on the Omnibus Frog Protection Act, which I so laboriously drafted for him, despite these recent attempts to encouragement:

—Congressman Paul McCloskey has promised to speak some words of encouragement to Waldie

—The Success Motivation Institute of Waco, Texas, has written Waldie, offering to design a special motivational course for him (offer spurned)

—the Old Southern Giant Bullfrog Farm of Evansville, Indiana, has written Waldie to throw the industry's support behind his efforts

—I have asked the legislative representative of the Defenders of American Wildlife to contact Waldie to get something started

—I have also asked Congressman William J. Scherle of Iowa to begin to prod Waldie by inserting a daily item

in the Congressional Record entitled, "Man's Inhumanity to Frogs—How Long?"
To date, even this upwelling of support and encouragement has made no discernible impact on this reprobate and two-time tergiversator.

It's time for the big guns, Art, and that of course means you.

Yours for frogs,

Nestle J. Frobish

ARTHUR HOPPE

February 16, 1972

Dear Nestle:
I can't understand it. I think perhaps that Waldie has gone power mad, and, in his insane desire to rule California as its next governor, has forgotten all about his friends—the frogs. Meanwhile, of course, frogs go on dying like flies. How long, oh Lord, how long?

Tergiversely yours,

Arthur Hoppe

Arthur Hoppe
San Francisco Chronicle/San Francisco/California

JEROME R. WALDIE
MEMBER OF CONGRESS
14TH DISTRICT, CALIFORNIA

WASHINGTON ADDRESS:
ROOM 409
CANNON HOUSE OFFICE BUILDING
WASHINGTON, D.C. 20515
PHONE: 225-9811
AREA CODE: 202

COMMITTEES:
JUDICIARY
POST OFFICE AND CIVIL SERVICE
SELECT COMMITTEE ON CRIME

DISTRICT REPRESENTATIVE
E. A. "PAT" FERGUSON
P.O. BOX 964
CIVIC CENTER
CONCORD, CALIFORNIA 94520
PHONE: 687-1200
AREA CODE: 415

RICHMOND OFFICE:
3915 MACDONALD AVENUE
RICHMOND, CALIFORNIA 94805
PHONE: 233-4425

Congress of the United States
House of Representatives
Washington, D.C. 20515

February 25, 1972

Mr. Nestle J. Frobish
Worldwide Fair Play for Frogs Committee
Lyndonville, Vermont 05851

Dear Nestle:

Although I did miss the boat on P. L. 92-159, I am not entirely to blame. I was not present on the floor at the time of the vote because of a conference with an outraged Department of Interior official on the Omnibus Frog Protection Act. For all the progress made at that conference I should have stayed on the floor—if not at home.

The choice given me between sand pits, frogs or doing nothing at all is not an easy one though the last alterna-

FAIR PLAY FOR FROGS

tive appeals most strongly whenever I receive one of your disturbed letters.

Sincerely yours,

Jerry Waldie

JEROME R. WALDIE
United States Congressman
Fourteenth District

JRW/ml

JEROME R. WALDIE
MEMBER OF CONGRESS
14TH DISTRICT, CALIFORNIA

WASHINGTON ADDRESS:
Room 408
Cannon House Office Building
Washington, D.C. 20515
Phone: 225-5511
Area Code: 202

COMMITTEES:
JUDICIARY
POST OFFICE AND CIVIL SERVICE
SELECT COMMITTEE ON CRIME

DISTRICT REPRESENTATIVE:
E. A. "Pat" Ferguson
P.O. Box 964
Civic Center
Concord, California 94520
Phone: 687-1200
Area Code: 415

Richmond Office:
3915 Macdonald Avenue
Richmond, California 94805
Phone: 233-4425

Congress of the United States
House of Representatives
Washington, D.C. 20515

March 16, 1972

Mr. Nestle J. Frobish
Lyndonville, Vermont 05851

Dear Mr. Frobish:

I have in hand your letter of February 5th, with the attachment of February 16th from that noted columnist, Arthur Hoppe.

FAIR PLAY FOR FROGS

Mr. Hoppe's letter states: "Meanwhile, of course, frogs go on dying like flies. . . ."

It does seem to me that we are putting the cart before the horse, so to speak, with the intense concern that you have been expressing relative to the condition of frogs, when it is apparent that flies are equally in jeopardy.

I am sorely tempted to leave off championing the cause of frogs and shift my efforts to the cause of flies. The latter are most numerous, let alone more fragile, and therefore in greater jeopardy.

Sincerely yours,

JEROME R. WALDIE, M. C.

JRW: afs
CC: Art Hoppe

WORLDWIDE FAIRPLAY FOR FROGS COMMITTEE

MAIN OFFICE
LYNDONVILLE, VERMONT
• •
OVERSEAS OFFICE
REDCOATS GREEN, ENGLAND

DISTRICT OFFICES
BERKELEY, CALIF.
MARTINEZ, CALIF.
SANTA CRUZ, CALIF.
NEW HAVEN, CONN.
CAMBRIDGE, MASS.
AUSTIN, TEXAS
WASHINGTON, D.C.

Lyndonville, Vt. 05851

March 28, 1972

Hon. Jerome Waldie
House Office Building
Washington, D. C.

Dear Congressman Waldie:

It can be said with certitude that, to the extent flies are dying, they are dying like flies.

I wish to point out, in case you have not noticed the fact, that one reason that flies are dying like, well, flies is that they are being devoured by the humble frog. In view of your dark history of frog hatred, Congressman, your sudden passion for flies suggests that you now wish to exterminate frogdom not by the massive use of gigs, napalm, and flamethrowers, etc., but by depriving the humble frog of his principal food supply. Is there no end to your iniquity?

Perhaps I should be thankful that you are turning to less depraved methods, but I must say that starvation is a long and unpleasant way to die; perhaps even your advocacy of slingshot warfare against the humble frog is more humane.

But let the issue be not beclouded. The issue is the

FAIR PLAY FOR FROGS

salvation of the frog. I readily concede that your vigorous efforts in behalf of the humble frog will not be particularly missed if you switch your attention to the even humbler fly, in view of the notable lack of success or even activity evident to date; but I would only suggest to you that you explore the depth of pro-fly sentiment before switching sides on this issue. According to the old proverb, "Frogs have friends, but flies, foes." It is worth remembering. Especially if you are still planning to ride a now-invisible groundswell to the governorship of California.

You may be edified also to recall the other relevant proverb, "Don't fool with a frog freak." An added virtue of recalling this gem is that, after saying it rapidly ten to fifteen times every morning, your tongue is limber enough to speak unerringly out of all sides of your mouth, an indispensable art to those seeking public office.

Get busy, please.

Nestle J. Frobish

Nestle J. Frobish

cc: Arthur Hoppe, Frogdom's Friend of the Fourth Estate

JEROME R. WALDIE
MEMBER OF CONGRESS
14TH DISTRICT, CALIFORNIA

WASHINGTON ADDRESS:
ROOM 408
CANNON HOUSE OFFICE BUILDING
WASHINGTON, D.C. 20515
PHONE: 225-5511
AREA CODE: 202

COMMITTEES:
JUDICIARY
POST OFFICE AND CIVIL SERVICE
SELECT COMMITTEE ON CRIME

DISTRICT REPRESENTATIVE:
E. A. "PAT" FERGUSON
P.O. BOX 864
CIVIC CENTER
CONCORD, CALIFORNIA 94520
PHONE: 687-1200
AREA CODE: 415

RICHMOND OFFICE:
3915 MACDONALD AVENUE
RICHMOND, CALIFORNIA 94805
PHONE: 233-4425

Congress of the United States
House of Representatives
Washington, D.C. 20515

April 4, 1972

Mr. Nestle J. Frobish
Lyndonville, Vermont 05851

Dear Mr. Frobish:

On a recent trip to San Diego, while speaking to a huge crowd of enthusiastic supporters, I was approached by a young man conveying the best wishes to me of Nestle J. Frobish.

He was aware that I had not been able to unearth your "cover," and was most reluctant to assist me in that continuing effort.

However, inadvertently he did mention that you were a state legislator, and when I suggested that you must be then a senator from the state of Vermont, his silence I construed as acquiescence. As you can see, I am closing in and expect to have full information as to your background in the very near future, at which time I will be able to ascertain with certainty whether your alleged commitment to the cause of frogs is in reality a personal commitment or a sham. Frankly, I have reason to suspect the latter.

By the way, when do you come up for reelection, and what is the name and address of your opponent?

Sincerely yours,

Jerry Waldie

JEROME R. WALDIE, M. C.

JRW:afs
CC: Mr. Art Hoppe

WORLDWIDE FAIRPLAY FOR FROGS

MAIN OFFICE
LYNDONVILLE, VERMONT
*   *
OVERSEAS OFFICE:
REDCOATS GREEN, ENGLAND

COMMITTEE

DISTRICT OFFICES:
BERKELEY, CALIF.
MARTINEZ, CALIF.
SANTA CRUZ, CALIF.
NEW HAVEN, CONN.
CAMBRIDGE, MASS.
AUSTIN, TEXAS
WASHINGTON, D.C.

Lyndonville, Vt. 05851

April 17, 1972

Honorable Jerome Waldie
House Office Building
Washington, D. C.

Dear Congressman Waldie:

Since you mention your experience in San Diego, wherein a person purporting to know me accosted you on the street, I feel compelled to reveal all.

The person accosting you on the street, according to well-placed sources in San Diego who are friendly to frogs, was actually an undercover agent for Jack Anderson, who followed you to San Diego, far from your own congressional district, to gather evidence on your role as intermediary between John Mitchell, ITT, and Rep. Bob Wilson. I am told this will emerge in a forthcoming Anderson column. I think it is diabolically clever of Mitchell, Wilson, and ITT to engage as an intermediary a person who is (a) a Democrat and (b) incapable of sustained effort in any kind of cause, as revealed by your prolonged lethargy in the matter of frogs. These characteristics, well known to the public, will no doubt shield you from suspicion—until the story breaks, of course.

I have discussed this expose with highly placed persons on Jack Anderson's staff who happen to be friendly to frogs. I suggested that before they break this scandal, thus terminating your ephemeral career, you be given one last chance to redeem your past sins as a frog-hater. They agreed. Introduce the Omnibus Frog Protection Act tomorrow—not only as a contribution to frogs everywhere, but as an investment in the continued marginal viability of your political career! If you do not act quickly, I am not sure I can hold this off. Everyone on Anderson's staff, incidentally, has agreed to deny ever having heard of me, or having investigated you in San Diego, in case an inquiry is made. Please don't embarrass them by asking.

In the meantime, I think that listening to the enclosed LP record, *Sounds of North American Frogs*, will make you fully aware of the frog problem. I am sure you will want to play the section "Diversity in Mating Calls" again and again, especially during mating season. Perhaps the sweet voices of the humble frog will win you over where my compelling logic and earnest entreaty has produced only mockery and inaction. Perhaps you will want to play it on the floor of the House, during what I understand are frequent lulls in the proceedings. I am sure you would get a terrific response if you did.

Persistently,

Nestle J. Frobish

Nestle J. Frobish

WORLDWIDE FAIRPLAY FOR FROGS COMMITTEE

MAIN OFFICE:
LYNDONVILLE, VERMONT
*   *
OVERSEAS OFFICE:
REDCOATS GREEN, ENGLAND

DISTRICT OFFICES:
BERKELEY, CALIF.
MARTINEZ, CALIF.
SANTA CRUZ, CALIF.
NEW HAVEN, CONN.
CAMBRIDGE, MASS.
AUSTIN, TEXAS
WASHINGTON, D.C.

Lyndonville, Vermont 05851
April 17, 1972

Mr. Arthur Hoppe
Friend of Flies
San Francisco Chronicle
San Francisco, California 94119

Dear Art:

You've got to be kidding. But if you are really setting up a Fair Play for Flies Committee, let him who has spearheaded the Committee to Outlaw Dumdum Bullets, Committee to Prohibit the Taking of Passenger Pigeons by Garotte, Friends of the Rann of Cutch, and the Worldwide Fair Play for Frogs With or Without Morton Sobell Committee, give you a piece of advice.

Don't count on Waldie for any help.

I have come to the conclusion, Art, that Waldie's seeming lack of rapport for frogs, to put it generously,

FAIR PLAY FOR FROGS

stems from inadequate familiarity with them. I have thus sent him the positively marvelous record *Sounds of North American Frogs*, distributed in the public interest by the National Wildlife Federation. I am sure he will find the section on mating calls very stimulating. I only hope it does not impel him to crawl up on the back of someone like Bella Abzug in a heedless moment. Congress is in enough trouble without having to explain that.

I am, incidentally, beginning to prepare a sequel to the above named record, entitled *Sounds of North American Frog-Lovers*. It will basically be a compelling soliloquy by me, punctuated from time to time by the sound track from the 1968 Democratic National Convention—Informal Proceedings in Grant Park. This one can't miss, Art.

Novus Ordo Seculorum,

Nestle J. Frobish

Nestle J. Frobish

JEROME R. WALDIE
MEMBER OF CONGRESS
14TH DISTRICT, CALIFORNIA

WASHINGTON ADDRESS:
ROOM 408
CANNON HOUSE OFFICE BUILDING
WASHINGTON, D.C. 20515
PHONE: 225-5911
AREA CODE: 202

COMMITTEES:
JUDICIARY
POST OFFICE AND CIVIL SERVICE
SELECT COMMITTEE ON CRIME

DISTRICT REPRESENTATIVE:
E. A. "PAT" FERGUSON
P.O. BOX 864
CIVIC CENTER
CONCORD, CALIFORNIA 94520
PHONE: 687-1200
AREA CODE: 415

RICHMOND OFFICE:
3915 MACDONALD AVENUE
RICHMOND, CALIFORNIA 94805
PHONE: 233-4425

Congress of the United States
House of Representatives
Washington, D.C. 20515

April 25, 1972

Mr. Nestle J. Frobish
Lyndonville, Vermont 05851

Dear Mr. Frobish:

In examining the statutes of Vermont, I conclude there is a law forbidding state senators to adopt a fictitious name and forbidding them to pretend they are someone better than they are in fact.

I believe you are in violation of the spirit if not the fact of that exemplary law.

I have listened to your LP, *Sounds of North American Frogs*, along with Mrs. Waldie. Neither I nor she was turned on by that recording.

I am enclosing a news article from my district indicating that, despite my alleged lethargy in the matter of advocacy of your cause, my leadership in this matter is producing results.

FAIR PLAY FOR FROGS

Can you indicate a similar step forward in the Vermont high school circles? I suspect not.

Sincerely yours,

[signature]

JEROME R. WALDIE, M. C.

JRW:afs
enc.

FROG VS. WARRIOR IN CAMPUS BATTLE

Concord, California   (AP)—A powerful subversive force is shaking the very foundations of hallowed tradition at Ygnacio Valley High.

A group calling itself FROG (Federation Recognizing Openmindness and Goodness) is seeking to unseat the school's mascot, the mighty warrior, and replace him with a passive frog.

Proclamation authors John Gelifin and Craig Weintraub—having garnered enough signatures for an election—will put the astonishing proposal to an all-school vote Thursday.

If the proposal passes—and there's a chance it will—the official school mascot will henceforth be Kermit the Frog (of Sesame Street), the school song will be Joy to the World, school colors will be dark green and lime green and freshmen will be known as Polywogs, sophomores as Tadpoles, juniors as Frogs, seniors as the all-mighty Bullfrogs.

The radical proclamation has already engendered a minor revolution on campus, with "movement" types pitted against "rah-rah" types.

FROG supporters have blanketed the school with leaflets—"One small vote for Kermit . . . a giant leap

FAIR PLAY FOR FROGS

(ha ha) for Ygnacio Valley"; "Mom, apple pie and the frog next door"—and the FROG proclamation has become the subject of vigorous debate in the daily *Bulletin* and in classrooms throughout the school.

"If this passes, I'll croak," said student Jennie Helmer last week. Other detractors angrily point out that the word "frog" is actually a derogatory term for Frenchmen.

But Craig and John—engineers of the present school government, American Field Service officers and members of the Student Mobilization Committee—justify their proclamation in the name of tolerance, love, peace, originality and creativity.

"In a world full of racism," the proclamation states, "where nigger is exchanged for black, Wop for Italian, and Kike for Jew, these nicknames subconsciously are derogatory and promote racism. So is the case of the Warrior and Indian, although maybe to a lesser degree. A frog is truly offensive to no one (they really don't spread warts). With segregation being advocated by our president and such personalities as George Wallace, perhaps the frog can be Ygnacio's weapon to combat the rampant racism which exists today."

The authors also point to the aggressive and hostile qualities embodied in the mascots of other high schools in the Diablo Valley Athletic League: Playton Valley "Eagles," Pittsburgh "Pirates," College Park "Falcons," Mount Diablo "Devils," Pleasant Hill "Rams," Antioch "Panthers," Pacifica "Spartans," Concord "Minutemen."

"In our move to counter violence," John and Craig explain, the symbol of a passive little frog will spread joy, love and peace throughout the entire Mount Diablo Unified School District."

They also hope the frog mascot will help to counter society's trend toward bureaucracy and standardization.

FAIR PLAY FOR FROGS

"The frog is a chance for originality, creativity and true beauty . . . The frog will put a block in the way of conformity and uniformity; it will give our school a chance to be unique and to be remembered."

PAUL N. McCLOSKEY, JR.
11TH DISTRICT, CALIFORNIA

COMMITTEE ON
GOVERNMENT OPERATIONS
AND
COMMITTEE ON
MERCHANT MARINE
AND FISHERIES

Congress of the United States
House of Representatives
Washington, D.C. 20515

April 26, 1972

Mr. Nestle J. Frobish
Lyndonville, Vermont 05851

Dear Nestle:

Knowing of your inability to persuade Congressman Waldie to do the right thing by frogs, I am enclosing a newspaper clipping from the San Francisco *Chronicle* of March 27, 1972.

The clipping describes a major frog war in Malaysia. Should this conflagration spread, as many claim it will, we will be faced with communist frogs in San Francisco. If they are not defeated in Southeast Asia, then one may look upon Congressman Waldie in future years as having been the Neville Chamberlain of his day.

FAIR PLAY FOR FROGS

I can only hope and pray that you will call this matter to Congressman Waldie's attention with your usual pithy suggestions and concise legislative recommendations.

Respectfully,

Paul N. McCloskey, Jr.

PNMcC:mm
Enclosure

MALAYSIAN FROGS AT WAR

Penang, Malaysia Mar. 26. (AP)—Two species of frogs battled for five hours yesterday, an event local residents believe portends a coming disaster but which zoologists say is a fight for breeding grounds.

Fisherman Osman Bin Mahmud, 54, reported that he was attracted to the scene of the frog war at about 6 a.m., when he heard loud croaking.

Osman said a dark brown and a yellow-skinned species were involved, and about 70 died in the battle.

WORLDWIDE FAIRPLAY FOR FROGS COMMITTEE

MAIN OFFICE
LYNDONVILLE, VERMONT
• •
OVERSEAS OFFICE
REDCOATS GREEN, ENGLAND

DISTRICT OFFICES
BERKELEY, CALIF.
MARTINEZ, CALIF.
SANTA CRUZ, CALIF.
NEW HAVEN, CONN.
CAMBRIDGE, MASS.
AUSTIN, TEXAS
WASHINGTON, D.C.

Lyndonville, Vt. 05851

May 6, 1972

Hon. Jerome Waldie
House Office Building
Washington, D. C.

Dear Congressman Waldie:

I beg to inform you that there is no law in this state forbidding state senators "to pretend that they are someone better than they are in fact." As a former state legislator you will recognize the absurdity of such a law. If a man is not allowed to pretend that he is better than he is in fact, how could he possibly remain in the state senate? Or be elected to any office? The right of a man to pretend he is better than he really is is the rock upon which our great system of representative government is founded. Any attempt by you to undermine this principle would be, if successful, instantly suicidal.

In any case, I am not a state senator. If I were a state senator—and as a matter of fact I am seriously considering running for it this year, as it would give me a more prestigious platform to speak out for frogdom—I would already have national recognition for my gallant efforts to save the frog.

I have learned to expect that even the most exciting renditions of frog voices are not likely to turn you on, but I cannot understand why the record had so little effect on Mrs. Waldie.

I am investigating the pro-frog activities at Ygnacio Valley High. This sounds good. I do not, however, see any evidence of your fine hand at work. I would expect you to favor renaming the high school teams the "Swamp Rangers" or some such.

Frog-lovers everywhere are praying for an end to your perversity.

Yours truly,

Nestle J. Frobish

Nestle J. Frobish

WORLDWIDE FAIRPLAY FOR FROGS COMMITTEE

MAIN OFFICE
LYNDONVILLE, VERMONT
*   *
OVERSEAS OFFICE:
REDCOATS GREEN, ENGLAND

DISTRICT OFFICES
BERKELEY, CALIF.
MARTINEZ, CALIF.
SANTA CRUZ, CALIF.
NEW HAVEN, CONN.
CAMBRIDGE, MASS.
AUSTIN, TEXAS
WASHINGTON, D.C.

Lyndonville, Vt. 05851
April 28, 1972

To: Congressman Paul McCloskey Jr.
Congressman William Hathaway
From: Nestle J. Frobish
Re: Your friend Waldie

A week ago I sent to Congressman Waldie, the faint-hearted friend of frogs, a magnificent record by the National Wildlife Federation, entitled *Sounds of the Frog.*

FAIR PLAY FOR FROGS

The part called "Diversity in Mating Calls" was particularly good and I am sure will serve as some inspiration to Congressman Waldie.

I know Congressman Waldie will be delighted with this gift and will be pleased if you would ask him to play it for you. Perhaps you could get a group of pro-frog solons together and have a real fun thing in Mr. Waldie's office. This is the kind of support he badly needs.

WORLDWIDE FAIRPLAY FOR FROGS COMMITTEE

MAIN OFFICE
LYNDONVILLE, VERMONT
*   *
OVERSEAS OFFICE
REDCOATS GREEN, ENGLAND

DISTRICT OFFICES:
BERKELEY, CALIF.
MARTINEZ, CALIF.
SANTA CRUZ, CALIF.
NEW HAVEN, CONN.
CAMBRIDGE, MASS.
AUSTIN, TEXAS
WASHINGTON, D.C.

Lyndonville, Vt. 05851

June 21, 1972

Hon. John Dingell
House Office Bldg.
Washington, D. C.

Dear Congressman Dingell:

Your insertion of an editorial entitled "The Wisdom of the Frog" has been brought to my attention from the Congressional Record, and I congratulate you for sharing this fine piece with your colleagues.

There is one man in the Congress who aspires to leading the fight to protect and preserve the humble frog. That man is your colleague, Jerome Waldie of California.

FAIR PLAY FOR FROGS

Eleven years ago Mr. Waldie, while a California Assemblyman, introduced a bill which read: "Frogs may be taken by using a slingshot." For eleven years I have worked patiently to get him to repent of his past sins, and he is almost to the point of doing so.

He needs your help. Please go to Waldie and tell him that you admire the wisdom of the frog and believe that frogs should be protected. I am sure you will be amazed at his delight in knowing he is not as alone as he thinks.

With a little encouragement from you, Waldie can become the friend of frogs he wants to be deep down inside, but for which role he has yet to muster the necessary inspiration.

Yours truly,

Nestle J. Frobish

OUTRAGE INFINITE !

DISGRACE UNSPEAKABLE !

WALDIE MUST ACT !!!

WORLDWIDE FAIRPLAY FOR FROGS
COMMITTEE

MAIN OFFICE
LYNDONVILLE, VERMONT
* *
OVERSEAS OFFICE
REDCOATS GREEN, ENGLAND

DISTRICT OFFICES
BERKELEY, CALIF.
MARTINEZ, CALIF.
SANTA CRUZ, CALIF.
NEW HAVEN, CONN.
CAMBRIDGE, MASS.
AUSTIN, TEXAS
WASHINGTON, D.C.

Lyndonville, Vt. 05851

June 21, 1972

Rep. Jerome Waldie
House Office Building
Washington, D. C.

Dear Congressman Waldie:

Outrage infinite! Disgrace unspeakable! See attached.

I can only assume that the nefarious frog-murderers of your district are behind this sinister plot to poison the minds of Americans against the humble frog.

"I can't believe I ate the whole thing!" Can you imagine?

He who would become a fully shriven Friend of Frogs, and who is in a position of national responsibility and prestige, and who is long overdue in these matters, must ACT. That, of course, means you.

An amendment to the Omnibus Frog Protection act, forbidding the transportation of films derogatory to frogs in interstate commerce should be a good beginning, especially if accompanied by your thundering declamations. I assume you have a large inventory of thundering declamations, inasmuch as you have used them very sparsely on behalf of the humble frog over the past eleven years.

FAIR PLAY FOR FROGS

The world is waiting! You must leap into the fray at once!

Urgently,

Nestle J Frobish

Nestle J. Frobish

WORLDWIDE FAIRPLAY FOR FROGS COMMITTEE

MAIN OFFICE:
LYNDONVILLE, VERMONT

* *

OVERSEAS OFFICE:
REDCOATS GREEN, ENGLAND

DISTRICT OFFICES:
BERKELEY, CALIF.
MARTINEZ, CALIF.
SANTA CRUZ, CALIF.
NEW HAVEN, CONN.
CAMBRIDGE, MASS.
AUSTIN, TEXAS
WASHINGTON, D.C.

Lyndonville, Vt. 05851
October 16, 1972

Defenders of Wildlife
Washington, D. C.

Dear Defenders:

I was recently solicited for a contribution to your organization.

Before contributing I should like to know what you are doing to protect the humble frog.

Everybody is familiar with the old maxim, "Everybody talks about savings frogs, but nobody does anything about it." I am trying to do something about it. Are you?

In particular, what action have you taken to publicize the efforts of Rep. Jerome Waldie (D-Calif.) to legalize additional methods of killing frogs? Admittedly this was eleven years ago, when he introduced the notorious Frog Murder Bill in the California legislature. Since then he professes to have repented, but yet refuses to take any initiative in protecting the humble frog.

Somebody has to get to Waldie. Will your organization do this?

How many supporters do you have in the 14th C.D. of California?

Yours truly,

Nestle J. Frobish

Nestle J. Frobish
Chairman

WORLDWIDE FAIRPLAY FOR FROGS COMMITTEE

MAIN OFFICE
LYNDONVILLE, VERMONT
•   •
OVERSEAS OFFICE
REDCOATS GREEN, ENGLAND

DISTRICT OFFICES
BERKELEY, CALIF.
MARTINEZ, CALIF.
SANTA CRUZ, CALIF.
NEW HAVEN, CONN.
CAMBRIDGE, MASS.
AUSTIN, TEXAS
WASHINGTON, D.C.

Lyndonville, Vermont 05851
October 16, 1972

Rep. Jerome R. Waldie
House Office Building
Washington, D. C. 20515

Dear Waldie:

I learn from the Washington *Post* that you are avidly supporting George McGovern for President, even as you disavow his "gutter tactics" in likening the current President to Hitler.

Since you are so enamored of Senator McGovern, it may be well to recall that the good senator is reputedly a staunch supporter of fair play for frogs. I enclose a copy of a leaflet distributed by his supporters prior to the

FAIR PLAY FOR FROGS

1972 California primary in which Senator McGovern comes out foursquare for frogdom and, specifically, the Worldwide Fair Play for Frogs Committee. This was forwarded to me by the Students for a Better Society at the University of California, Santa Cruz, a highly active and public-spirited group.

Now, with your presidential candidate thus on the record, how can you lag behind? When Senator McGovern turns to you and says, "Jerome, why haven't you introduced the Omnibus Frog Protection Act of 1972?" how are you going to face him?

I am sure you would like to keep this explosive issue out of the papers on the eve of your reelection bid. So let's get with it. Before I call Senator McGovern and tell him the bad news about you.

Expectantly,

Nestle J. Frobish

Nestle J. Frobish

P.S.: If you will send me the name and address of your Republican opponent, I will seek out his views on the frog issue.

WORLDWIDE FAIRPLAY FOR FROGS COMMITTEE

MAIN OFFICE
LYNDONVILLE, VERMONT
* *
OVERSEAS OFFICE:
REDCOATS GREEN, ENGLAND

DISTRICT OFFICES:
BERKELEY, CALIF.
MARTINEZ, CALIF.
SANTA CRUZ, CALIF.
NEW HAVEN, CONN.
CAMBRIDGE, MASS.
AUSTIN, TEXAS
WASHINGTON, D.C.

Lyndonville, Vt. 05851

October 18, 1972

School Newspaper
Ygnacio Valley High School
Concord, California

LETTER TO THE EDITOR

The students of your high school are to be congratulated for their fine organization, Federation Recognizing Openness and Goodness (FROG) and for recommending that the school's mascot be the humble frog.

Your students may be interested to know that their very own Congressman, Jerome Waldie, has for many years been a notorious hater of frogs.

As an assemblyman in 1961, Waldie introduced the notorious Frog-Murder Bill, A. B. 2301, which read: "Frogs may be taken by using a slingshot." Fortunately, cooler heads prevailed and the bill did not pass.

Congressman Waldie has never sincerely abandoned his animosity for the humble frog.

A large and indignant delegation of Ygnacio Valley students protesting Waldie's inhuman attitude at one of his campaign gatherings might well have quite an impact on his thinking. Especially if there are many inventive signs carried and the press is duly notified.

FAIR PLAY FOR FROGS

This man should be made to answer for his sins. What better time than now? And what better people than the members of FROG [Federation Recognizing Openness & Goodness] to force the issue?

Sincerely,

Nestle J. Frobish

Nestle J. Frobish
Friend of Frogs

The National Observer
Week Ending December 30, 1972

Letters on Nuclear Plants, a Defense of Frogs,
and Other Concerns

To the Editor:

After reading your good feature on nuclear power plants, I find myself at a loss to explain the depravity of this Toby Bocanegra of Gary, Indiana.

Mr. Bocanegra, your readers will recall, is the Gary union official who hates frogs. "These ecology creeps," Mr. Bocanegra solemnly avers, "are running around spending thousands of somebody's dollars just to save a swamp full of frogs."

Mr. Bocanegra has obviously never taken time off from a hard day of sticking it to the ecology creeps to ponder the contributions to mankind of the humble frog. Genial, inoffensive, cheerful, he crouches in his aqueous lair (the humble frog, not Mr. Bocanegra) and gives us the pleasant chuggarummm of a summer's evening.

Alas, the humble frog, friend of mankind, may well be on the way out. I would just as soon lose Mr. Bocanegra, plus his nuclear power station, plus his labor union, plus all of Gary, Ind.

Nestle J. Frobish
Chairman
Worldwide Fair Play for Frogs Committee
Lyndonville, Vt.

CC: Arthur Hoppe

A R T H U R   H O P P E

January 2, 1973

Dear Nestle:

I wish, with all my heart, that Mr. Bocanegra be transformed into a frog prince. Only in that form will he realize the plight of our warty friends. May he travel the highways of the earth, hopping from town to city, looking for a kiss to turn him back to a union official.

I promise to keep that in mind over my next wishbone. Happy New Year,

Arthur Hoppe
San Francisco Chronicle/San Francisco/California

JEROME R. WALDIE
MEMBER OF CONGRESS
14TH DISTRICT, CALIFORNIA

WASHINGTON ADDRESS:
Room 408
CANNON HOUSE OFFICE BUILDING
WASHINGTON, D.C. 20515
PHONE: 225-5911
AREA CODE: 202

COMMITTEES:
JUDICIARY
POST OFFICE AND CIVIL SERVICE
SELECT COMMITTEE ON CRIME

DISTRICT REPRESENTATIVE:
E. A. "PAT" FERGUSON
P.O. Box 964
CIVIC CENTER
CONCORD, CALIFORNIA 94520
PHONE: 687-1200
AREA CODE: 415

RICHMOND OFFICE:
3915 MACDONALD AVENUE
RICHMOND, CALIFORNIA 94805
PHONE: 233-4425

Congress of the United States
House of Representatives
Washington, D.C. 20515

January 4, 1973

Mr. Nestle J. Frobish
Lyndonville, Vermont 05851

Dear Mr. Frobish:

Your letter to the NATIONAL OBSERVER was one of the few of recent date with which I find myself in thorough agreement. Perhaps I should exclude from that pattern of thought agreement with your belief that "all of Gary, Indiana" should also be exchanged for the protection of the humble frog.

Though I would be willing to lose Mr. Bocanegra, his nuclear power station, and his labor union, I have some reservations about all of Gary, Indiana.

Sincerely yours,

JEROME R. WALDIE, M. C.

JRW:afs

WORLDWIDE FAIRPLAY FOR FROGS COMMITTEE

MAIN OFFICE
LYNDONVILLE, VERMONT
*   *
OVERSEAS OFFICE
REDCOATS GREEN, ENGLAND

DISTRICT OFFICES
BERKELEY, CALIF.
MARTINEZ, CALIF.
SANTA CRUZ, CALIF.
NEW HAVEN, CONN.
CAMBRIDGE, MASS.
AUSTIN, TEXAS
WASHINGTON, D.C.

Lyndonville, Vt. 05851

January 10, 1973

Berkeley Friends of Frogs
University of California
Berkeley, California

Dear Wes and Kathe:

Rarely has such a famous friend of frogs as Frobish found such fabulous fellow frog fanciers as you! The letterhead is magnificent! Your goals are noble! Your initiative outstanding! Your genius dazzling! And you probably look like Paul Newman and Raquel Welch, respectively, as well. (If this last conjecture is close to the truth, Kathe, please send photo of yourself in or nearly in a bikini, preferably knee deep in a swamp, and I will announce you as Frog Queen of '73 with attendant publicity.)

As to your fine program for action:

1) It is slightly immodest of me to urge you to seek the naming of College Five for me, Nestle Frobish, but, as I wrote Governor Reagan last year, "if the Board of Regents decides to name College Five after me, I want you to know that I accept." This letter has strangely gone unanswered. I suppose letters to the governor and regents and editorials in the student papers would be a good start.

FAIR PLAY FOR FROGS

2) Put the heat on Waldie! Tell me more, incidentally, about our Martinez chapter, which is in Waldie's district. Last year there was a movement at Ygnacio Valley High School out around Concord to rename their athletic teams the "Frogs" instead of the purple avengers or something. I wrote with words of praise and encouragement, mentioning that their congressman was the notorious frog-murderer and suggesting a little political action, but no response. Perhaps you'd like to make a chapter field trip and arouse these youth.

3) We have missed National Frog Protection Week, alas, so let's wait until next year.

4) History of frogdom requires some scholarship. All I can supply are some small tidbits, such as the statement of St. Basil (4th century) that "At the command of God the waters were gifted with productive power; from slime and muddy places, frogs, flies and gnats came into being." While this seems to reveal Divine Origins for frogs, I could do without the part about the flies and gnats. Perhaps there is a professor of zoological history at UC who would assign a research paper on this subject.

5) Again, you need a legislative sponsor. Perhaps Senator Moscone, who I understand is contemplating a race for governor in '74, possibly against Waldie. This would give him a splendid chance to lock up the frog issue, given Waldie's past record. Should I send him a stirring letter?

6) We could add the national emblem change to the Omnibus Frog Protection act as another section—if we can get Waldie moving.

7) I really like the idea of putting a frog on the Board of Regents. Several years ago the voters of one state in Brazil elected a hippopotamus to the state legislature, so there is some precedent. Not to mention the incumbent

FAIR PLAY FOR FROGS

turkeys. "Multiple ornithoptera demand singular rana" might be a rallying cry; or, "Put a frog on the board or the whole state will go up in flames!" (this version appeals to the less literate).

I hope all this helps. I am confident that with all your initiative this will develop into a mass movement equivalent in irresistible force to the sinking of half your fair state into the ocean next March, or whenever.

VITALLY IMPORTANT: Please send me about fifty sheets of that splendid letterhead!

Incidentally, you might seek some publicity through Arthur Hoppe of the *Chronicle,* who has written about me and frogs on at least three occasions in years past (when I was head of the Santa Clara County FPFC).

Right on!

Nestle Frobish

Nestle Frobish

Mr. Jeff Wells
Students for a Better Society
Santa Cruz, Calif.

Dear Jeff:

One of our nationwide legion of fellow-leapers has reminded me that the Calaveras Jumping Frog Jubilee is nigh upon us.

Recalling your heroic work in last year's contest, in the face of a shameful bias against dinky frogs, I thought you might be ready for an encore.

What about entering a frog named "Jerome R. Waldie" that has been trained to simulate catatonia on command? This would demonstrate and dramatize Waldie's penchant for inactivity in the cause of the humble frog.

FAIR PLAY FOR FROGS

Or perhaps you could enter a vicious frog-eating great blue heron, disguised as a frog, named "Jerome R. Waldie" to dramatize the penchant Waldie has for murdering frogs.

How about a traveling exhibit of slingshots, napalm canisters, flame throwers, nerve gas ampules, etc. with appropriate literature portraying Waldie as what he is?

Or maybe a huge frog float mounted on a flat-bed trailer with appropriate exhortations displayed thereon, which could be driven around the site to good advantage. Skywriting by an airplane disguised as a huge frog?

In any case, I know your fertile mind will produce some device to get the frog nationwide sympathy while bringing the opprobrium of mankind down upon the "Killer Congressman."

Onward and upward,

Nestle J. Frobish

Nestle J. Frobish

Jerome R. Waldie
TESTIMONIAL

Committee:
  Hon. 'Tip' O'Neill
    House Majority Leader, Mass.
  Hon. William D. Hathaway
    U. S. Senator, Maine

Dear Friend:
Jerry Waldie is special—and April 3rd is a special night.

Perhaps not all of us hold that specialness to the same degree or in the same way—depending how closely we have been privileged to know and work with him. But, in a real sense, he is special to all of us who look for rare qualities of excellence and spirit in public life and who, when they are found, seek to honor the meaning as well as the man.

In this spirit, few commend themselves to our own sense of respect, generosity and dedication as does Jerry Waldie. Through the difficult seasons of war and domestic neglect his deep dedication to civil liberties, the genuine needs of people in terms of health and hope, and his efforts to reform our institutions to better serve our most noble aspirations takes on special significance. For all those moments of quiet courage and adherence to principle, Jerry Waldie stands as one of the best examples of our prologue to a more hopeful future.

This testimonial reception and buffet, to be held Tuesday, April 3rd, at the Quality Inn—Capital Hill, 415 New Jersey Ave., N.W., from 6:00 to 9:00 p.m.—honors Jerry Waldie as he closes one chapter of his public service. Neither he nor we, among his many friends, colleagues, well-wishers and admiring adversaries, can say what the future will bring, but it is our purpose to gather now in honor of the man himself as we have come to know him and for all the many accomplishments, moments of inspiration, and examples of lonely courage he has already given us through the difficult seasons of the last decade. In honoring him, we also reaffirm for ourselves the values in public life we most cherish and which are most deserving of real honor.

Won't you join us—for Jerry, for ourselves, and for the future? We think you, too, will find it means something "special."

Sincerely,
The Committee

FAIR PLAY FOR FROGS

(While the proceeds of this event are not required to be
reported under the Federal Election Campaign Act of
1971, The Committee will file a report with the Clerk of
the House and the Secretary of State of the State of California.)

WORLDWIDE FAIRPLAY FOR FROGS COMMITTEE

MAIN OFFICE
LYNDONVILLE, VERMONT
* *
OVERSEAS OFFICE
REDCOATS GREEN, ENGLAND

DISTRICT OFFICES
BERKELEY, CALIF.
MARTINEZ, CALIF.
SANTA CRUZ, CALIF.
NEW HAVEN, CONN.
CAMBRIDGE, MASS.
AUSTIN, TEXAS
WASHINGTON, D.C.

March 18, 1973

EMERGENCY BULLETIN!!!

To: All Frog-Lovers
From: Nestle J. Frobish, Chairman, WFPFC
Subject: Outrage infinite! Infamy unspeakable!

Can you imagine—a bunch of Washington low-lifers
have actually organized a testimonial dinner for *America's
leading Frog-Murderer,* Congressman Jerome Waldie!

The same Jerome Waldie who sponsored the infamous
Frog Murder bill of 1961, which read: "Frogs may be
taken by using a slingshot."

The same Jerome Waldie who has steadfastly refused

FAIR PLAY FOR FROGS

to introduce the Omnibus Frog Protection Act in the congress!

The same Jerome Waldie who, in an uncharacteristic moment of candor, has admitted that he is a secret shareholder in the Jerry Waldie All-Steel Gig and Slingshot Works!

Not only this, but these blackguards have decorated the invitation (enclosed) with Our Symbol, the Humble Frog, across whose breast is inscribed the loathesome words, "We like Congressman Waldie."

Friends and Frog-Lovers—we must Act! Do you have friends in college or high school in or around Washington? Can you alert them to this outrage, and ask them to picket the Quality Inn at 6:00 p. m. on April 3, with all appropriate signs? We should turn out at least a hundred intrepid marchers!

Time is of the essence! Write, wire, call, ESP—anything! This outrage must not pass unnoticed and unchallenged. The World demands Justice—and who does the World look to in this matter, if not us Friends of Frogs?

Hysterically,

Nestle

Nestle

P.S. If you have a frog suit, wear it!

March 31, 1973

Sen. William Hathaway
Senate Office Building
Washington, D. C. 20510

Dear Senator Hathaway:

Thank you for inviting me to attend the first annual Jerry Waldie Celebration Festival on April 3. Unhappily,

FAIR PLAY FOR FROGS

my responsibilities as the world's most outspoken friend of frogs prevent my attendance in person. As you are aware, Mr. Waldie has a very, very spotty record with respect to frogs, which I am sure is of concern to you, now that you have roared into the Senate fresh from the frog-bejeweled Allagash. Nevertheless, on this occasion I am willing, in that spirit of magnanimity for which I am occasionally known, to offer the following tribute to Mr. Waldie which you may read on the occasion of the dinner:

It is indeed a wholly unexpected pleasure for me to be able to say a few words about Congressman Jerome Waldie. In describing his achievements on behalf of the humble frog, I must confess that words almost fail me. His character is well known to all, and cannot be rated too highly. His convictions are a matter of record, which will remain long after he is gone. He is a man of the most exiguous talents. He is a man whose personal habits have been widely emulated by part of the nation's population. Whenever an emergency has arisen, whenever mass confusion has developed, whenever morale has suffered a precipitous decline, Congressman Waldie has almost invariably been found at the center of things, displaying his customary energy, imagination, and reliability. And tonight, as we gather to catapult Jerry Waldie into the forefront of American politics, we can only be reminded of the wise words of the great American philosopher, E. J. Underdunk, who once said, "Sometimes you win, sometimes you lose."

Let us hope that this great leap forward for Jerry Waldie will materialize into a great leap forward for frog-

FAIR PLAY FOR FROGS

dom. There is, of course, not much reason to believe this, but anyone can hope.

Sincerely,

Nestle J. Frobish

Nestle J. Frobish

P.S.: Don't forget to read this at the dinner.

The Evening Star and Daily News
Washington, D. C., Wednesday, April 4, 1973

PITY POOR FROGS

by Judy Flander
Star-News Staff Writer

To get into the testimonial reception for Rep. Jerry Waldie, D-Cal., last night one had to cross a picket line of frog-lovers in front of the Quality Inn. According to legend, about 10 years ago, when Waldie was a state legislator, he introduced a bill that made it legal to kill frogs with a slingshot in California.

Representatives of the Worldwide Fairplay for Frogs Committee, headed by the also legendary Nestle S. Frobish, about 15 young people, all but five American University students, carried protest signs: "Waldie hates frogs," "God help the frogs" and "Waldie repent."

A spokesman, who said his organization was pushing a Senate omnibus frog protection act revealed that the committee plans to ask California Gov. Ronald Reagan to name a frog to the University of California Board of Regents.

Meanwhile, inside, in a murky, red-walled room, supporters of Waldie for governor of California gathered to share a buffet of hard-boiled eggs, olives and cheese dip.

FAIR PLAY FOR FROGS

For $100 apiece, it was hardly a feast but there was plenty of hard liquor and fun.

One of the cosponsors, the mythical Dick Tuck, said he was sorry he was late. "But I had to pay off the pickets. They wouldn't take a check." He passed around green stick-on frog labels, some of which said, "God help Jerry Waldie."

Rep. Morris Udall, D-Ariz., who in another incarnation must have been Mark Russell, introduced a star-spangled roster of guests starting with Speaker of the House Carl Albert.

"We plan to have for you a debate between Maxine Cheshire and Frank Sinatra on the roll of stability and clean living in American life," said Udall, introducing Sen. William Hathaway, D-Maine, who recently defeated veteran Sen. Margaret Chase Smith.

"There is not much I can tell you about campaigning," Hathaway said to Waldie. "I might be able to tell you more if you were running against a woman."

Many of Waldie's colleagues showed up, including one unlikely pair, Reps. Pete McCloskey, D-Calif. and John Rousselot, R-Calif.

Introducing Rousselot from the tiny corner platform, Udall said, "Here he is, fresh from a meeting of the Young Americans for Freedom."

McCloskey took the platform next: "If a man can't be compassionate about frogs, how can we trust him with the governorship of California?"

Straight from New York, through the auspices of Susan Cohen, who works for former Rep. Allard Lowenstein, came folksinger Peter Yarrow to sing "This Land Is Our Land," and—for Joanne and Jerry Waldie's daughter and son-in-law, Jill and Eric Becraft—"Weave Me the Sunshine." Yarrow quietly insisted on quiet and got it.

FAIR PLAY FOR FROGS

Both California senators, Alan Cranston and John Tunney, were there along with other California representatives including Ron Dellums (whose wife Roscoe was a cosponsor of the testimonial), John McFall and Don Edwards.

WORLDWIDE FAIRPLAY FOR FROGS COMMITTEE

MAIN OFFICE
LYNDONVILLE, VERMONT
• •
OVERSEAS OFFICE:
REDCOATS GREEN, ENGLAND

DISTRICT OFFICES
BERKELEY, CALIF.
MARTINEZ, CALIF.
SANTA CRUZ, CALIF.
NEW HAVEN, CONN.
CAMBRIDGE, MASS.
AUSTIN, TEXAS
WASHINGTON, D.C.

Nestle J. Frobish
Chairman

Lyndonville, Vt. 05851

April 10, 1973

Hon. Paul N. McCloskey, Jr.
House Office Building
Washington, D. C.

Dear Congressman McCloskey:
Please accept the congratulations of frog-lovers everywhere for your penetrating and incisive, indeed holophrastic, observation, made during the Waldie Testimonial Cocktail Hour, otherwise known as the Frog-Murder Follies. Truly, if a man cannot be compassionate toward frogs, can he be a compassionate leader of his fellow human beings?

FAIR PLAY FOR FROGS

I am enclosing a copy of the famous "Omnibus Frog Protection Act of 1971," which your shameless colleague Mr. Waldie failed to introduce. In your position as ranking member of the Subcommittee on Fish and Wildlife Conservation of the House Merchant Marine and Fisheries Committee, you are certainly in a key position to inspire Mr. Waldie to take the Great Leap and introduce this bill. I know you will make it a special point to persuade this backsliding reprobate that the time is Now!

Also enclosed is a copy of the Waldie Frog-Murder Bill of 1961 which hopefully can be used among your colleagues to generate a little pressure on this infamous ranaphobe.

Godspeed,

Nestle J. Frobish

Nestle J. Frobish

April 10, 1973

Mr. Gary Nurenberg
Capital Fair Play for Frogs Committee
Silver Spring, Md.

Dear Gary:

Tidings of your spectacular demonstration outside the Waldie reception have reached me and I congratulate you on the magnificent success of your spectacular undertaking!

Frogdom certainly has a fearless new friend in you!

The reverberations of this epic confrontation will rattle the cattails in every swamp in America!

Please convey my extreme good wishes and felicitations to all those stalwart friends of frogs who told their story to an eager world on that glorious occasion!

Onward and upward,

Nestle J. Frobish

Nestle J. Frobish

WORLDWIDE FAIRPLAY FOR FROGS COMMITTEE

MAIN OFFICE
LYNDONVILLE, VERMONT
* *
OVERSEAS OFFICE:
REDCOATS GREEN, ENGLAND

DISTRICT OFFICES:
BERKELEY, CALIF.
MARTINEZ, CALIF.
SANTA CRUZ, CALIF.
NEW HAVEN, CONN.
CAMBRIDGE, MASS.
AUSTIN, TEXAS
WASHINGTON, D.C.

April 19, 1973

To: All Chapters

From: Your Humble Chairman

Our relentless campaign to persuade so-called Congressman Jerome Waldie to befriend the humble frog is building up irresistible pressure.

On April 3 a group of closet frog-haters around Washington put on a Waldie for Governor of California cocktail party. Our alert American University chapter was there in full force with about a dozen devastating picket signs which, according to chapter chairman Gary Nurenberg, "caused congressmen and passersby to freak out."

FAIR PLAY FOR FROGS

A Jack Anderson reporter present asked House Speaker Carl Albert what he intended to do about Waldie's stand on frogs. The Speaker replied, "I'm not aware of how my colleague stands on frogs." That's the problem, Carl . . .

A local radio pundit has offered to "do whatever is necessary" to promote the frog cause. I will be writing a few pro-frog and anti-Waldie editorials for his station. (I dare Waldie to seek equal time!)

Congressman Paul McCloskey of California has promised to urge Waldie to get moving, and assured early hearings on the Omnibus Frog Protection Act. Since McCloskey is ranking member of the House Fish and Wildlife Conservation Subcommittee, this is an indication of support in powerful quarters.

Keep up the good work, gang! We are on the threshold of great and wonderful happenings!

Nestle J Frobish

May 4, 1973

Mr. H. R. Haldeman
The White House
Washington, DC

Dear Mr. Haldeman:

I understand from the media reports that you have recently been the center of some unfavorable publicity. I am writing to suggest a unique and exciting method for restoring and improving your all-important public image.

A man in your position of power, indeed, in charge of the President of the United States, could scarcely have failed to notice the sorry plight of American frogs. To be sure, the crisis of frogdom has not made the headlines to the degree other issues have—like Viet Nam, inflation, unemployment, the Wa . . ., well, you know, other issues. But it is no less real.

Now my suggestion is this: with all that cash in your office safe you are in a position to make a really big contribution to further the work of the Worldwide Fair Play for Frogs Committee. Not only would this help our efforts, but it would associate you in the public mind with two Master Concepts—the Frog, and Fair Play. And it would also relieve you of the embarrassment of having all that money in the office safe, which a lot of nosy reporters seem to find awfully interesting.

So what do you say? I am ready to organize a splendid national press conference to announce that "Haldeman Backs Fair Play for Frogs." I know this will make every paper in the country.

Enthusiastically,

Nestle J. Frobish

Chairman

P.S.: In the off chance you aren't interested, could you forward this letter to Mr. Stans or Mr. Kalmbach?

WORLDWIDE FAIRPLAY FOR FROGS COMMITTEE

MAIN OFFICE
LYNDONVILLE, VERMONT
*   *
OVERSEAS OFFICE:
REDCOATS GREEN, ENGLAND

DISTRICT OFFICES
BERKELEY, CALIF.
MARTINEZ, CALIF.
SANTA CRUZ, CALIF.
NEW HAVEN, CONN.
CAMBRIDGE, MASS.
AUSTIN, TEXAS
WASHINGTON, D.C.

Nestle J. Frobish
Chairman

Lyndonville, Vt. 05851

May 7, 1973

Rep. Jerome Waldie
House Office Building
Washington, DC

Dear Congressman Waldie:

It has come to my attention that another three months have gone by without your having done anything for frogs, unless it can be said that your refraining from mass murder during that period constitutes some kind of contribution. I am also told by my far-flung legion of pro-frog operatives that your scandalous indolence on frog matters was forcibly brought to the attention of certain of your colleagues and other misguided well-wishers who turned out at a combination booze party and orgy for the supposed benefit of your incipient gubernatorial campaign on April 3. We friends of frogs sleep not, but remain permanently a-bristle with indignation at your antics.

But, in my famous tradition of continuing to deal with the unwashed and unshriven, which I picked up from Father Damien, I have a couple of new opportunities for you to vindicate yourself.

FAIR PLAY FOR FROGS

First there is the matter of the proposed International Convention on Trade in Certain Species of Wildlife, which is now open for signing. Listed in Appendix I (Really Endangered Species) is only the "Golden Frog," which, I am told, inhabits the high marshes of Tannu Tuva, where the natives revere it as God. In Appendix II (Damn Near Endangered Species) appears only the Sonoran Green Toad, which is not even a frog. Considering that Appendix I includes such other creatures with far smaller constituencies as the Scaley-Tailed Possum, the Queensland Hairy Nosed Wombat, the Volcano Rabbit, Mongolian Beaver, Hook-billed Hermit, Indian Wild Ass, and (God save us all!) Abbott's Booby, it seems to me even a modest effort on your part should be able to get a dozen or so species of American frogs onto the list. Or if not in Appendix I, at least in Appendix II, along with the Virgin Island Screech Owl, the Gila Monster, and the Jackass Penguin. All of which, by the way, seem to have their counterparts in congress.

In addition to this exercise, you might use your self-styled ability to add some explicit protection for the humble frog to S. 1592, the Administration's endangered species bill, which in its present form goes to great lengths to avoid mentioning frogs.

I must add that I regard your efforts to portray yourself as a friend of the environment—by your puffery about Mrs. LeConte's effort to save Palos Verdes Peninsula—as wholly without foundation in fact. In view of the recent events in the Capitol revolving about allegations of duplicity in high places, I should think you would be making a special, though unaccustomed, effort to appear as a creature of probity, integrity, and reliability. Remember— someday the Washington *Post* won't have Nixon to kick around anymore, and you may be next on their list.

FAIR PLAY FOR FROGS

Incidentally, for what it may be worth, there is the possibility that the Worldwide Fair Play for Frogs Committee may receive substantial funding in the near future. I recently wrote Mr. H. R. Haldeman, late of the President's palace guard, pointing out that his contribution of all the remaining cash in his office safe to the WFPFC would at one stroke remove that cash as a matter of interest to many reporters, and revitalize his image as a friend of all living things, which has not been coming through very strongly in recent news reports. I have not yet had a reply to this offer but am waiting hopefully. Just to maximize our chances here, I added in my letter that if he didn't feel he could accept this fine offer, he should forward my letter to Mr. Stans and Mr. Kalmbach who are reportedly similarly situated.

If you have occasion to put in a good word for us with Mr. Haldeman, please do so.

Yours,

Nestle J. Frobish

ARTHUR HOPPE

May 7, 1973

Dear Nestle:

I'm ever so reassured to know that you're right up there, fighting for frogs, righting wrongs, and generally trying to make the best out of every situation. I think there is a good chance that Mr. Haldeman will climb aboard the

frog bandwagon, in his anxiety to join a winning team.
Gratefully,

Arthur Hoppe
San Francisco Chronicle/San Francisco/California

JEROME R. WALDIE
MEMBER OF CONGRESS
14TH DISTRICT, CALIFORNIA

WASHINGTON ADDRESS:
Room 408
CANNON HOUSE OFFICE BUILDING
WASHINGTON, D.C. 20515
PHONE: 225-5911
AREA CODE: 202

COMMITTEES:
JUDICIARY
POST OFFICE AND CIVIL SERVICE
SELECT COMMITTEE ON CRIME

DISTRICT REPRESENTATIVE:
E. A. "PAT" FERGUSON
P.O. BOX 864
CIVIC CENTER
CONCORD, CALIFORNIA 94520
PHONE: 687-1200
AREA CODE: 415

RICHMOND OFFICE:
3915 MACDONALD AVENUE
RICHMOND, CALIFORNIA 94805
PHONE: 233-4425

Congress of the United States
House of Representatives
Washington, D.C. 20515

June 27, 1973

Mr. Nestle J. Frobish
Lyndonville, Vermont 05851

Dear Mr. Frobish:

I have not been overly impressed of late with suggestions from you as to actions I should take to advance the prospects for endangered or otherwise frogs.

But in your May 7th letter you suggest an endeavor that does interest me.

I am inquiring as to where the proposed International Convention on Trade in Certain Species of Wildlife will be held. And, if it is to be held in a desirable location with ample opportunity for relaxation from the arduous pursuit of justice and fair play for frogs, I intend to attend, providing my trip and attendant expenses will be paid for by an appropriate committee.

I do not desire to comment on your frivolous references to Watergate. I am still uncertain as to your true identity and would not be overly surprised to learn you are engaged in surveillance activities or in "dirty tricks." There is much about you that leaves me uneasy.

Sincerely,

JEROME R. WALDIE, M. C.

JRW:afs

November 1, 1973

Hon. Jerome Waldie
House Office Building
Washington, D. C.

Dear Congressman Waldie:

I have just returned from a most invigorating tour of frog habitats and other fascinating places, not including the international convention you mentioned, however, and can report that the cause of frogdom was never stronger. I can also report considerable disgust with your lack of leadership in protecting the humble frog, but what else is new?

The cause of frogdom took a major leap forward with House passage of H. R. 37, the Endangered and Threatened Species Conservation Act. This act explicitly includes amphibians, which includes the object of our affection, frogs. I note that you voted in favor of this act. Heat getting to you, hey, Jerome?

I also notice that you have sponsored not the Omnibus Frog Protection Act, but an act to guarantee the right of frog-murderers to stalk the wetlands of federally-funded reservoirs impaling helpless frogs with gigs, presumably manufactured by the Jerry Waldie All-Steel Gig Works. I refer of course to H. R. 9673. You didn't dare come out and state "frog killing," using instead the euphemisms "maximization of project hunting, fishing, and *other outdoor recreation benefits.*" Don't think I'm not watching. We friends of frogs never sleep. Your ruse of asking the impeachment of President Nixon to divert attention from this monstrous bill will not work either.

Incidentally, I am informed that a lunatic is stumbling about southern California claiming to be you, running for governor. You will want to do something about this, I'm sure, before it makes you more of a laughingstock than you already are. I can, of course, rescue you from this sorry condition, if you will just introduce the Frog Protection Act. I'll arrange a shriving on network TV, complete with such friends of frogs as Maharaj Ji, H. R. Haldeman, Rev. Ike, Ed Reinecke, Joe Alioto, Bob Moretti, Arthur Hoppe, and maybe even Linda Lovelace as Mistress of Ceremonies. All you have to do is ask!

Perpetually yours,

Nestle J. Frobish

JEROME R. WALDIE
MEMBER OF CONGRESS
14TH DISTRICT, CALIFORNIA

WASHINGTON ADDRESS:
Room 408
Cannon House Office Building
Washington, D.C. 20515
Phone: 225-5911
Area Code: 202

COMMITTEES:
JUDICIARY
POST OFFICE AND CIVIL SERVICE
SELECT COMMITTEE ON CRIME

DISTRICT REPRESENTATIVE:
E. A. "Pat" Ferguson
P.O. Box 984
Civic Center
Concord, California 94520
Phone: 687-1200
Area Code: 415

Richmond Office:
3915 Macdonald Avenue
Richmond, California 94805
Phone: 233-4425

Congress of the United States
House of Representatives
Washington, D.C. 20515

November 19, 1973

Mr. Nestle J. Frobish
Worldwide Fair Play for Frogs Committee
Lyndonville, Vermont 05851

Dear Mr. Frobish:

Despite your claims of continuous travel on behalf of your committee, I find it difficult to believe that you have ever left Lyndonville. Only a very informed person would realize that if Maharaj Ji, Haldeman, Rev. Ike, Reinecke, Alioto, Moretti, and Hoppe were on network television with Linda Lovelace, even the frogs would cry out in protest.

Sincerely yours,

JEROME R. WALDIE
Member of Congress

JRW/jp

May 29, 1974

Rep. Jermoe R. Waldie
House Office Building
Washington, D. C. 20515

Dear Jermoe:

It's probably too late.

After thirteen years of exhorting you to repent your anti-frog propensities, I gave up last January. Instead, I started telling Californians about A. B. 2301 and your unwillingness to be shriven therefor.

I pointed out that Moretti, Alioto, Brown, Roth, Flournoy and Reinecke, whatever else might be said of them, had an absolutely clean record when it came to persecuting frogdom.

The word does get around, Jermoe. I wouldn't be surprised if all of these guys outpolled you next Tuesday. There are millions of frog-lovers in California, and all of them vote. I think I pointed this out in these identical words some years ago in a letter to you, but you heeded not, and now you shall be elected not.

It's too late now to reverse this tide. Even if I were to go on statewide television and announce that Waldie had truly repented, introduced the Frog Protection Act, and been shriven, I doubt if anyone would take it seriously. NO argument there, right?

So let's look at your long-term plans. After you have voted to take President Whatisname (deleted), by slingshot or otherwise, you will probably have a month or two to introduce the Omnibus Frog Protection Act and build up a tidal wave of support for it. Perhaps your pal McCloskey can take up the cause in the next congress, if he survives the primary next week. I suppose that when

FAIR PLAY FOR FROGS

you leave Congress, you won't have ol' Frobe to kick you around any more.

Reminiscently,

Nestle J. Frobish

Nestle J. Frobish

JEROME R. WALDIE
MEMBER OF CONGRESS
14TH DISTRICT, CALIFORNIA

WASHINGTON ADDRESS:
Room 406
Cannon House Office Building
Washington, D.C. 20515
Phone: 225-5511
Area Code: 202

COMMITTEES:
JUDICIARY
POST OFFICE AND CIVIL SERVICE
SELECT COMMITTEE ON CRIME

DISTRICT REPRESENTATIVE:
E. A. "Pat" Ferguson
P.O. Box 864
Civic Center
Concord, California 94520
Phone: 687-1200
Area Code: 415

Richmond Office:
3915 Macdonald Avenue
Richmond, California 94805
Phone: 233-4428

Congress of the United States
House of Representatives
Washington, D.C. 20515

June 25, 1974

Mr. Nestle J. Frobish, Chairman
Worldwide Fair Play for Frogs Committee
Lyndonville, Vt. 05851

Dear Nestle:

You've done some outrageous things in the past thirteen years, Nestle, but this time you've really blown it.

In your own naïveté, you thought that campaigning against me for governor would further the cause of frogdom. Absolutely false!

Indeed, as the Democratic nominee for governor of

California, I would have had the necessary influence and power to push the Frog Protection Act through the Congress—and I might have been persuaded to do it!

But, now . . . and despite your fantasies, McCloskey will never do it. It's true, winning is better than losing—but an 800-vote mandate hardly augurs well for McCloskey's influence back here.

So, Nestle, it looks like you've outsmarted yourself once again.

Finally—and this is just hearsay—I understand that both the Democratic and Republican nominees for my Congressional seat served frogs' legs at their victory celebrations. Another step back for frogdom, if true.

I hope you do not keep in touch, Mr. Frobish. In the meanwhile you'll have to find a sport other than "let's kick Waldie around," to divert attention away from your incessant croaking, and to cover up your fumbling efforts.

Sincerely,

JEROME R. WALDIE, M. C.

JRW/dam

P.S. McCloskey insists you live in a pond. I find that easy to believe. Is it true?

July 2, 1974

Hon. Jermoe R. Waldie
House Office Building
Washington, D. C. 20515

Dear Jermoe:

I don't see why you are being so hard on me. After all, I am the only guy who has been paying much attention to you the past six months.

FAIR PLAY FOR FROGS

Who has outsmarted whoself? In six months you will not only not be governor of California, but you will also not be congressman. Indeed, you will most likely be unemployed, passing your many idle hours slogging through the swamps around Antioch zapping the humble frog with whatever weapon you currently favor for that purpose.

By contrast, I, Nestle J. Frobish, will still be the illustrious and intrepid Chairman of the Worldwide Fair Play for Frogs Committee.

I agree that come January there will be little reason for us to continue to try to reform you, Jermoe. The fight for frogdom will no doubt shift to other fronts. But I must confess that I will somewhat miss the supreme challenge of getting you squared away and shriven, or shrived, or shrove, or whatever it was. God forbid that I, Nestle J. Frobish, should get soft on frog-murderers, but now and then, located between your hard, vicious exterior and your heart of granite, I seemed to detect a miniscule annulus of decency and good humor. But perhaps I am getting soft.

While Congressman McCloskey's landslide victory and his great popularity among his fellow Republicans make him the next logical champion of the frog cause, I will bear in mind your admonition.

Please send your forwarding address next January so I can continue to make life miserable for you.

Yours,

Nestle J. Frobish

Nestle J. Frobish

WORLDWIDE FAIRPLAY FOR FROGS
COMMITTEE

MAIN OFFICE
LYNDONVILLE, VERMONT
* *
OVERSEAS OFFICE:
REDCOATS GREEN, ENGLAND

DISTRICT OFFICES
BERKELEY, CALIF.
MARTINEZ, CALIF.
SANTA CRUZ, CALIF.
NEW HAVEN, CONN.
CAMBRIDGE, MASS.
AUSTIN, TEXAS
WASHINGTON, D.C.

Nestle J. Frobish
Chairman

Lyndonville, Vt. 05851

August 4, 1974

GOOD NEWS, FROG LOVERS!

CONGRESSMAN JEROME WALDIE, the Mad Butcher of the Swamps, has been destroyed in his bid for governor of California. A terrific outpouring of frog-lovers sealed Waldie's fate in the June 4 Democratic primary, leaving him far down in the pack. Let this be a lesson to other frog-murderers who seek to climb to higher office over the carcasses of their helpless victims!

ANOTHER MISCREANT BROUGHT TO JUSTICE:

Rutland Daily Herald, Saturday morning, July 27, 1974

FROG FARMER IS SENTENCED ON TAX FRAUD

July 27—Clarence H. Mumley of Alburg was handed a one-year suspended prison sentence, placed on two years probation, and ordered to pay a $1,000 fine at his sentencing on income-tax fraud in U. S. District Court in Rutland Friday.

Mumley had earlier pleaded guilty to willful failure to file his 1968 federal income-tax returns.

FAIR PLAY FOR FROGS

Mumley is the owner and operator of the Lake Champlain Frog Farm in Alburg. That business sells live frogs throughout the United States for research purposes.

He is also liable for full payment of income taxes and penalties on civil assessments, which will be settled at a later time.

Mumley was represented by Atty. Lawrence Wright of Burlington, and the government was represented by Assistant U. S. Atty. William B. Gray.

Spurred on, no doubt, by President Nixon's tax slight-of-hand, another person of dubious character tried to bilk Uncle Sam of tax revenues. Is it any surprise that one is being impeached by Congress, and the other is a frog farmer? This may well be the Watergate of the anti-frog movement!

WE ARE STORMING AHEAD ON ALL FRONTS! Keep up the good work.

WORLDWIDE FAIRPLAY FOR FROGS COMMITTEE

MAIN OFFICE
LYNDONVILLE, VERMONT
* *
OVERSEAS OFFICE:
REDCOATS GREEN, ENGLAND

DISTRICT OFFICES:
BERKELEY, CALIF.
MARTINEZ, CALIF.
SANTA CRUZ, CALIF.
NEW HAVEN, CONN.
CAMBRIDGE, MASS.
AUSTIN, TEXAS
WASHINGTON, D.C.

Nestle J. Frobish
Chairman

Lyndonville, Vt. 05851

January 16, 1975
Honorable Paul N. McCloskey
House Office Building
Washington, DC 20515

Dear Congressman McCloskey:

As a fellow champion of the humble frog, you are no doubt delighted and relieved at the sullen departure from the House of the arch frog-murderer of our time, Jerome R. Waldie.

Only one thing remains to be done to efface his blot on the national escutcheon.

That is to push through the Congress the enclosed resolution which expunges his existence from the annals of our national government.

I am sure you will want to offer this with wide cosponsorship. In fact, I am already drafting a circular letter to your 434 colleagues telling them of the initiative you are planning to take in this measure, and exhorting their support for you.

I know this effort will help you to leap into the front

FAIR PLAY FOR FROGS

rank of congressmen devoted to decency, honor, and frogs.

Call on me if I can be of any further help.

Yours truly,

Nestle J. Frobish

Chairman

94th CONGRESS
1st SESSION

(Original signature of Member)

H. J. RES.

IN THE HOUSE OF REPRESENTATIVES

Mr. McCLOSKEY .... introduced the following joint resolution; which was

referred to the Committee on Censure ....

JOINT RESOLUTION
(Insert title of joint resolution here)

Resolved by the Senate and House of Representatives of the United States of America in Congress assembled, that in light of his imperious refusal to sponsor the Omnibus Frog Protection Act after asking to be shriven for his lifelong hostility to the humble frog, and for various low crimes and misdemeanors associated with his notorious and un-American anti-frog fetish, the record of service of former member JEROME R. WALDIE of California be expunged from the records of the Congress.

PAUL N. McCLOSKEY, JR.
11TH DISTRICT, CALIFORNIA

COMMITTEE ON
GOVERNMENT OPERATIONS
AND
COMMITTEE ON
MERCHANT MARINE
AND FISHERIES

Congress of the United States
House of Representatives
Washington, D.C. 20515

March 26, 1975

Mr. Nestle J. Frobish, Chairman
Worldwide Fair Play for Frogs Committee
Lyndonville, Vermont 05851

Dear Mr. Frobish:

It seems particularly important during the Easter season to forgive rather than to punish. I hope you will understand, therefore, that despite my repugnance for Congressman Waldie's dismal record and attitude toward frogs, I cannot bring myself to introduce a further resolution to censure him at this time.

I thought you might be interested in some related comments on Southeast Asia, an area where Congressman

FAIR PLAY FOR FROGS

Waldie has occasionally shown a dim perception of events
and trends.

Sincerely,

Paul N. McCloskey, Jr.

PNMcC:ww
Enclosures

WORLDWIDE FAIRPLAY FOR FROGS COMMITTEE

MAIN OFFICE
LYNDONVILLE, VERMONT
*   *
OVERSEAS OFFICE:
REDCOATS GREEN, ENGLAND

DISTRICT OFFICES:
BERKELEY, CALIF.
MARTINEZ, CALIF.
SANTA CRUZ, CALIF.
NEW HAVEN, CONN.
CAMBRIDGE, MASS.
AUSTIN, TEXAS
WASHINGTON, D.C.

March 31, 1975

Hon. Paul N. McCloskey
House Office Building
Washington, D. C. 20515

Dear Congressman McCloskey:

Now that Easter is safely past, and the world once
again abandons whatever manifestations of charity and
forgiveness may have been embraced during the Easter
period, I hope you will reconsider your decision not to
introduce the resolution expunging from the records of
Congress any mention of the mere existence of the Arch
Frog-Murderer, Jerome R. Waldie.

If, however, you continue to be overwhelmed by the
spirit of forgiveness, may I suggest a less drastic but still
appropriate course of action? Being a student of history,

you no doubt recall the outrage that suffused the citizens of Georgia when the notorious Yazoo frauds came to light in 1796. Every member of the Georgia legislature of 1795, save one, proved either to have an investment in the Yazoo land grants, or to have been bribed by those who did. The popular reaction was vehement. According to Dumas Malone, "So intent were the Georgians on removing from their record every trace of this outrageous transaction that they tore from the legislative journal the pages bearing on it, and by means of a microscope called down fire from Heaven to ignite them."

Perhaps instead of a formal motion to expunge, it would be possible to assemble the pages from the *Congressional Record* bearing the words of Jerome R. Waldie and call down a similar fate upon them. This would be an excellent occasion for some pro-frog speeches and, in view of the copious outpourings of print unloaded upon a hapless public by Waldie over the years, the volume might well be enough to roast some weenies and marshmallows for those attending. Please be sure to notify the press when this important and precedent-setting event has been scheduled.

I read your Viet Nam report with interest, but failed to note any discussion of the terrible havoc wrought on the frog population of that troubled land by the prodigious artillery fire documented therein. I am sure you will correct this oversight at an early occasion.

Yours truly,

Nestle J. Frobish

Nestle J. Frobish

WORLDWIDE FAIRPLAY FOR FROGS COMMITTEE

MAIN OFFICE
LYNDONVILLE, VERMONT
* *
OVERSEAS OFFICE:
REDCOATS GREEN, ENGLAND

DISTRICT OFFICES
BERKELEY, CALIF.
MARTINEZ, CALIF.
SANTA CRUZ, CALIF.
NEW HAVEN, CONN.
CAMBRIDGE, MASS.
AUSTIN, TEXAS
WASHINGTON, D.C.

March 31, 1975

Mr. Jerome R. Waldie
Bethesda, Maryland 20034

Dear Late Congressman Waldie:

At some point in your flagitious career of what you amusingly call "public service" you must have done some unspeakable favor for that pro-frog bayonet-wielding Marine, Congressman Paul McCloskey. That is the only explanation I can find for his unwillingness to introduce into the House the enclosed resolution, which would expunge any record of your service therein. In any case, I want you to know that efforts continue to make America a finer, nobler place by erasing from its annals your career of violence and perversity.

But be that as it may, I can report that Mr. Barry Vogel, our so-called agent, seems to be laboring manfully to get the Waldish-Frobie Papers (or whatever) into print. I hope he is successful in closing the deal soon, as I will need the money therefrom to counter the campaign of anti-frog terror that will doubtless be financed by your equal share of the proceeds therefrom.

I truly hope that your next stint of "public service" will be the fabrication of license plates alongside your pals Haldeman, Ehrlichman, and Mitchell, under circumstances where the frog population of the world will have little to fear from your continued ravages.

Yours enthusiastically,

Nestle J. Frobish

JEROME R. WALDIE
ATTORNEY-AT-LAW
100 INDIANA AVENUE N.W. - 8TH FLOOR
WASHINGTON, D. C. 20001
(202) 393-4664

April 4, 1975

Mr. Nestle J. Frobish
Worldwide Fair Play for Frogs Committee
Lyndonville, Vermont 05851

Dear Mr. Frobish:

Pursuant to my long-held and acted-upon commitment to candor, integrity and openness, I am enclosing a copy of my letter of complaint to the U. S. Postal Authorities concerning your nefarious conduct over these many years and your use of the U. S. mails in furtherance of your petty schemes to mislead and harass, if not defraud, your targets of abuse—myself being the most prominent among them.

Sincerely,

Jerome R. Waldie

JRW:laf
Enclosure

FAIR PLAY FOR FROGS

JEROME R. WALDIE
ATTORNEY-AT-LAW
100 INDIANA AVENUE N.W. - 8TH FLOOR
WASHINGTON, D. C. 20001
(202) 393-4664

April 4, 1975

U. S. Postal Authorities
Harassment, Abuse & Perhaps Fraud
   Investigation Section
L'Enfant Plaza
Washington, DC

Gentlemen:

For approximately eleven (11) years, one Nestle J. Frobish has been using the U. S. Mails to conduct a campaign of Harassment, Abuse and Perhaps Fraud of many unsuspecting citizens, myself being the most prominent among them.

Mr. Frobish purports to be the chairman of a fictitious organization named the Worldwide Fair Play for Frogs Committee. In fact, not only does this committee not exist, but Mr. Frobish, who unhappily, most assuredly exists, is using an alias. I do not know what his real name might be but, in another era of this correspondence time frame, suspected he was from behind the Iron Curtain. With the increasing success of détente, though, I have discarded that theory.

Though I have not personally been solicited for funds, I suspect many have, because some of our latter correspondence betrays on his part a strong and obvious propensity to financial greed and it is reasonable to assume that such, in fact, motivates his despicable conduct in this scheme.

My personal correspondence with him will amply confirm my charge of Abuse and Harassment. Harassment will be equally evident by a review of correspondence in my possession from Frobish to others.

Fraud I only suspect from the massive pattern of deception that attends this entire incident.

Please move quickly on this complaint. I know not what response will be forthcoming from him when he learns of this inquiry, but I fear his reaction will be intemperate and erratic.

Sincerely,

Jerome R. Waldie

JRW:laf

WORLDWIDE FAIRPLAY FOR FROGS COMMITTEE

MAIN OFFICE
YNDONV LLE VERMONT
* *
OVERSEAS OFFICE
REDCOATS GREEN, ENGLAND

DISTRICT OFFICES
BERKELEY, CALIF.
MARTINEZ, CALIF.
SANTA CRUZ, CALIF.
NEW HAVEN, CONN.
CAMBRIDGE, MASS.
AUSTIN, TEXAS
WASHINGTON, B.C.

Nestle J. Frobish
Chairman

Lyndonville, Vt. 05851

April 21, 1975

Mr. Benjamin F. Bailar
Postmaster General
U. S. Postal Service
Washington, D. C.

Dear Ben:

Your generous contribution to the committee is much appreciated. It is good to know that there are so many frog-lovers in high places.

I wouldn't ordinarily call this to your attention, but the renegade ex-congressman, Jerome R. Waldie, is now embarked on a campaign of intimidation against your Harassment, Abuse and Perhaps Fraud Investigation Section. He is alleging that he is the subject of all those things, all of which he richly deserves except fraud, which he is.

I trust you will inform the chief of this section to disregard Waldie's entreaties as the delusions of a perverted mind, which they are, if any.

His letter richly deserves the fate of the 500,000 Waldie for Governor letters which, if memory serves me correctly, are now sitting in a Postal Service warehouse in Kalispell, Montana, waiting for the price of recycled paper to rise. Thanks again for that one, Ben.

Yours truly,

Nestle J. Frobish

Nestle J. Frobish

INDEX

A

Albert, Rep. Carl, 57–58, 70, 79, 148
Alioto, Joseph, 155, 156, 157
Anderson, Jack, 113–4, 148
Ashbrook, Rep. John, 61–2, 70
Aspinall, Rep. Wayne, 72, 77, 78

B

Bailar, Benjamin F., 172–173
Becraft, Eric and Jill, 144
Berkeley Friends of Frogs, 135
Bilex, Bob, 84
Bocanegra, Toby, 132–4
Boggs, Rep. Hale, 58, 70, 80
Brown, Edmund G. Jr., 157

C

Calaveras Jumping Frog Jubilee, 137
Cardiff Giant, 28
Cherry, Allen, 100, 101–2, 103
Church, Sen. Frank, 97
Cohen, Susan, 144
Committee to Outlaw Dumdum Bullets, 3–5, 115
Committee to Prohibit Taking of Passenger Pigeons by Garotte, 9, 115
Cranston, Sen. Alan, 145

D

Defenders of Wildlife, 128–29
Dellums, Rep. Ron, 145
Dingell, Rep. John, 124–25

E

East Bay Committee for Fair Play to Frogs and Justice for Morton Sobell, 9
Edwards, Rep. Don, 145
Ehrlichman, John, 168

F

Federation Recognizing Openness and Goodness (FROG), 118–20, 131
Fenwick, Charles, 4
Five, Thurgood P., 96
Flander, Judy, 143
Flournoy, Houston, 157
Ford, Rep. Gerald R., 58–59, 70, 80
Friends of the Rann of Cutch, 115
Frobish, Nestle J.
    Decries U.S. non-ratification of 1899 Dumdum bullet convention, 3
    Proposes monster rides for kiddies, 6
    Discovers Waldie Frog Murder Bill, 9
    and Committee to Oppose the Hunting of Passenger Pigeons by Garotte, 9
    and East Bay Committee for Fair Play to Frogs and Justice for Morton Sobell, 9
    Challenges Waldie on Frog Murder Bill, 10
    Brands Waldie as Assassin!, 18

INDEX